The Real Deal *about* Your Meal

AF652154

The Real Deal *about* Your Meal

Power-up Your Plate *for a* Healthy Body & Blissful Living

Yogesh Singh

HAY HOUSE

HAY HOUSE INDIA
New Delhi • London • Sydney
Carlsbad, California • New York City

Copyright © 2022 Yogesh Singh

Hay House Publishers (India) Pvt Ltd
Muskaan Complex, Plot No. 3, B-2, Vasant Kunj, New Delhi – 110070, India

Hay House LLC, P.O. Box 5100, Carlsbad, CA 92018-5100, USA
Hay House UK Ltd, 1st Floor, Crawford Corner, 91-93 Baker Street, London W1U 6QQ, UK
Hay House Australia Publishing Pty Ltd, 18/36 Ralph St., Alexandria NSW 2015, Australia

Email: contact@hayhouse.co.in
Website: www.hayhouse.co.in

The views and opinions expressed in this book are the author's own and the facts are as reported by him. They have been verified to the extent possible, and the publishers are not in any way liable for the same.

All rights reserved. No part of this publication may be reproduced, by any mechanical, photographic, or electronic process, or in the form of a phonographic recording, nor may it be stored in a retrieval system, transmitted, or otherwise be copied for public or private use – other than for 'fair use' as brief quotations embodied in articles and reviews – without prior written permission of the publisher.

The author of this book does not dispense medical advice or prescribe the use of any technique as a form of treatment for physical or medical problems without the advice of a physician, either directly or indirectly. The intent of the author is only to offer information of a general nature to help you in your quest for emotional and spiritual well-being. In the event you use any of the information in this book for yourself, which is your constitutional right, the author and the publisher assume no responsibility for your actions.

First published by Hay House India, 2022
Reprint, 2026
11 10 9 8 7 6 5 4 3 2

ISBN 978-93-91067-13-7
ISBN 978-93-91067-29-8 (e-book)

Printed at Repro India Limited

FSC www.fsc.org MIX Paper from responsible sources FSC® C047271

Hay House is committed to a sustainable future for our business, our readers and our planet. This book is made from Forest Stewardship Council® certified paper.

To
My mother, Mrs Shashi Singh
My father, Mr Hari Nath Singh
My brother, Mr Shailesh Singh
My wife, Dr Sarita Singh
and
My biggest competitor and lovely son, Aaryaveer Singh

Contents

Introduction 11

Part I
Understanding the Health Components

1. A Healthy Lifestyle 15
2. Antioxidants—Superheroes of Nutrition 20
3. Prebiotics and Probiotics 33
4. Detoxification—A Boon 38
5. Weight Management 45
6. Rainbow Diet Is the Way to Go 64
7. Ayurveda—The Science of Healing from Within 73
8. Aphrodisiacs 81
9. Food Combinations 86
10. Vegetarianism vs Non-Vegetarianism 99
11. Microgreens 105

Part II
Superfoods

12. Onions 111
13. Flaxseeds 116
14. Beetroot 121

15. Garlic 125
16. Ginger 130
17. Curd 134
18. Turmeric 139
19. Fish 144
20. Eggs 149
21. Mushroom 154
22. Almonds 160
23. Spinach 165
24. Walnuts 169
25. Figs 173
26. Amla 177
27. Pomegranate 182
28. Jaggery 186
29. Carrots 190
30. Coconut 194
31. Sprouts 198
32. Guava 203
33. Wheatgrass 207
34. Curry Leaves 211
35. Dates 215

Health Mantras 220
Trivia 227
Bibliography 234
Acknowledgements 240

'To eat is a necessity, but to eat intelligently is an art.'

—François de la Rochefoucauld

Introduction

Mother Nature has blessed humankind with an array of incredible foods from both plant and animals. It has provided us with a colossal world of foods that we, till date, have not been able to explore all the benefits they have to offer.

The advancement of technology has led to a more comfortable lifestyle, which has also changed the framework of consuming food and selecting suitable diets. But this new era of a relaxed lifestyle has also led to an increase in several long-lasting ailments. The genesis of many diseases is due to the lack of exercise and unhealthy food habits, but this phase has also alarmed individuals to be more alert and cautious of what they consume. People are going back to the roots.

It is said that a healthy mind resides in a healthy body. Good food makes a person physically healthy, and in turn, the mind gets nourished. But there is a lot of misinformation out there, and sadly, many celebrities are promoting slimming teas and pills that do not have enough scientific evidence. Moreover, many are ignorant as to what should be consumed for one's overall health, and fall prey to such falsities.

In today's fast paced life, people are running short of time to cook food properly, and this has led to issues like malnutrition and inclination towards fast foods, which have their own side effects like obesity, cardiovascular diseases, etc. Moreover, many people suffer—or are at the risk of suffering—from genetic diseases, and a proper diet can eliminate many such risks. We cannot control our genetics, but we can control the way we nourish our bodies. Eating a healthy diet, along with exercising routinely, is one of the most important things we can do to reduce the risk of developing chronic issues like diabetes, heart disease, and cancer.

People prefer organoleptic quality over therapeutic values of food ingredients. This situation is highly alarming and need to be dealt with the right and appropriate knowledge. People have also been using certain buzzwords like antioxidants, detoxification, probiotics, keto diet, aphrodisiacs, etc., without understanding the actual concepts behind them. The state of ignorance and stupefaction must be enlightened so that humanity could inherit optimum benefits. This book is an attempt at spreading knowledge so that the readers can decide the good and bad for themselves.

This book is divided into two parts—Understanding the Health Components and Superfoods. The former is the soul of the book that concentrates on spreading awareness regarding the finer dimensions of healthy foods and diets.

On the other hand, the second part is the heart of the book, and it focuses on the nutritional aspects of certain foods and their benefits.

I have tried my best to decode all the finer aspects of health in a simple and lucid language. The aim for the book is to gift all readers the in-depth knowledge about the benefits of following a nutritious diet plan not only for weight loss or weight maintenance but for holistic wellness.

Your body is your temple, and it deserves more than processed and fast foods that would only hamper the quality of your life. My reason for writing this compendium is to inform every reader about what they are consuming—the good, the bad, and the ugly—so that they could make an effort to ameliorate their food habits, which would, undoubtedly lead to a happier and healthier life.

Part I

UNDERSTANDING THE HEALTH COMPONENTS

1
A Healthy Lifestyle

'Those who think they have no time for bodily exercise will sooner or later have to find time for illness.'

—Edward Stanley

Lifestyle, an assemblage of two keywords—life and style—is a frequently used term by all. The concept of a lifestyle encompasses certain things in its periphery and is defined by understanding the core values of all such things in its circumference.

Keeping in mind the simplistic understanding of a lifestyle, it simply reflects the manner of living outlined by a definite set of values and attitudes. These values are fitness, exercise, positive approach, nutrition, body posture, stance, mindset, etc. Nevertheless, people generally associate lifestyle with luxury or simplicity but ignore the most important type of lifestyle, i.e. healthy lifestyle.

It is never late to incorporate good values in life. Many people are forced to adapt a healthy lifestyle as they are suffering due to certain ailments. The concept of healthy lifestyle should be incorporated early on, if possible. If this is attained, it would, undoubtedly, diminish the possibility of diseases that would arise later in life. An aware and cognizant mind adapts the culture of healthy lifestyle easily. Most importantly, if a child incorporates the habit of healthy eating, i.e. avoiding junk food and exercising, the possibility of obesity and related issues decreases. Thus, it won't be an exaggeration to state that a healthy lifestyle is the foundation of disease-free life.

Positive Approach

The positivity of thought or positive approach is the base of all conviction and belief of a lifestyle. We have been hearing the word 'positivity' every so often. But what is it all about? Positivity is basically a quality or state of mind portrayed by affirmation and assertiveness, requiring no proofs or evidences. It erupts in a healthy state of mind. Positivity is characterised by optimism, energy, happiness, appreciation, fertile ideas in mind, and brilliance in life, whereas negativity is characterised by pessimism, destructiveness, languidness, gloominess, condemnation, barren mind, and darkness in life.

So, first and foremost, for anyone to lead a healthy lifestyle, the person has to be positive in their approach.

The positive attitude can be attained by adopting simple principles in life. In order to achieve this one should have faith in self and belief in supreme almighty; along with huge sense of optimism. One should indulge in activities that are close to their heart like painting, dancing, reading, cooking, watching movies, imitating others in light mood, gardening, etc. or explore the creative aspects, if any, as well. One should support the art of giving or sharing rather than expecting from others. One also should develop a sense of humour, a sense of appreciation in spite of criticising and blaming others. Apart from this, one should take initiative in shouldering responsibility and along with build an atmosphere of team work. One should try to help others as much as possible rather than being complainant what have they in their life. This all should be topped with light exercise and physical activity.

Fitness

No one can lead a good lifestyle without having fitness in their life. A fit and healthy body can enjoy every aspect of life and can truly relish life's pleasures. Money can't buy health. An expensive bed cannot be a source of sound sleep if one is experiencing pain in one's back.

Exercise

Lately, there has been a huge trend towards being fit. Fitness is something everyone dreams of. Many succumb to their sluggish lifestyle and give up, but there are a few who make working out a discipline. Exercise does not only gift one with good health but boosts one's confidence as well.

Even light exercises can prove to be quite beneficial like few minutes of brisk walk, cycling, dancing, aerobic exercise, Zumba, yoga, etc. Physical activities are associated with better cognitive learning, improved way of thinking, better sense of judgement, decrease in anxiety and stress, and anti-ageing. It is also helpful in managing weight, boost blood circulation, and improve the functioning of the respiratory organs.

Regular exercise is associated with improved bone density and a better brain alignment. Exercising regularly also aids in strong and healthy muscles. People who exercise are more energetic than those who do not.

Exercise has many benefits that can't be ignored:

- It improves the overall aura of the personality
- It boosts confidence and reduces stress
- It makes the person more focus- and result-oriented
- It improves immunity

- It delays ageing
- It helps the person to be more jovial, motivated, and, most importantly, make them active in all aspects of their life
- It promotes better sex life
- It creates better coordination between brain and memory
- It improves the quality of sleep

Nutrition

It won't be an exaggeration to say that the present era is the most nutrition-conscious era. A few terms like nutrients, calorie, calorie burn, weight-management, and obesity are commonly heard and discussed nowadays. Healthy and nutritious food is highly demanded and consumed across all breadth and length of the globe.

Stance

Stance is another word for body posture. Posture, if rightly maintained, shows, improves, and exudes confidence, whereas incorrect body posture leads to pain in certain areas of the body—especially the back and neck—in the long run. A right stance keeps flexibility in the muscles and even prevents joint problem. People usually correlate body posture with body language, but both are entirely distinct aspects.

Mindset

Generally, there are two types of mindset—healthy and diseased. If a person thinks about themselves as unwell, they will definitely get ill. So, a person must believe in good things and have faith. One should refrain from criticising others. Criticising anyone is the one thing that hardly gains anyone anything in their life but takes away the most important thing—time. Criticising others has many side effects like deterioration of a relationship, downfall of the image of the person doing so, and so on. It is mandatory for all to be happy in their life, whatsoever they have or don't have in their life. This factor would help them remain healthy as well.

A healthy lifestyle is not merely a way of life but is the need of the hour due to its multiple benefits. Undoubtedly, a positive approach to this lifestyle not only safeguards us from numerous diseases but helps in leading a life that is worth living. It eliminates one's dependency on medicines. So, gift yourself a life that is healthy by adopting the above-mentioned principles. After all, life is not just about breathing and existing in this universe, but its quality, too, plays a significant role.

2

Antioxidants—Superheroes of Nutrition

'Antioxidants are really like little bodyguards inside your body that protect your cells from disease.'

—Cynthia Sass

Current ages have witnessed several trends flourishing, and the awareness regarding wellness is among one of them. Certain terms have been used commonly in this context and 'antioxidants' is, undoubtedly, one such word. It can be said that antioxidant is a household term and used as if *à la mode*.

Antioxidants are powerful substances that counteract the widespread ill effects of free radicals and make our body safe and strong from oxidative stress damage. Antioxidants are beneficial to our body as they remove and neutralise the free radicals from our bloodstream. Antioxidants protect the healthy cells by killing the free radicals that are harmful for our body.

People use the term antioxidants without understanding the core essence of it. Hence, it is essential to explore what they are in simplest possible language. In order to understand antioxidants in a better way, we need to understand few basic key terms such as cell, free radicals, and oxidants first.

Cell is the most fundamental structural and functional units of all living organisms. The body's cells produce energy by using oxygen. In this process, at times, the oxygen reacts with certain body compounds and forms highly unstable molecules. These highly reactive and unstable molecules are known as free radicals. Free radicals are formed due to results of oxidative damage. They are quite dangerous to body tissues and are considered to be the cause for diseases like cancer, dementia, heart issues, decline in immunity, and premature ageing.

Actually, free radicals are unstable substances as they contain unpaired electrons in it. Free radicals capture electron from other substances to pair its unpaired electrons to get stable. In this process, free radicals become stable but, in turn, makes other substances unstable, which are, again, free radicals. Thus, many unstable free radicals are formed due to this chain reaction, harming the body.

Free radicals have the capacity and temperament to attack healthy cells, leading to several disorders such as cell damage and various diseases mentioned above. It is believed to be the reason for around 50 diseases like cancer, dementia, Alzheimer's, Parkinson's, asthma, male fertility issues, high blood pressure, atherosclerosis, heart stroke, diabetes, inflammatory disorders, fatigue, etc.

Free radical formations are also due to factors such as energy metabolism, diabetes, acute illness, obesity, breakdown of medicine consumed, injuries, air pollution, high levels of oxygen, radiations, tobacco smoke, UV rays, and so on.

This is where the superhero antioxidants come into play as they counteract the villainous effects of free radicals or oxidative damage. Antioxidants are widely distinct, and due to their varied characteristics, it impart distinct benefits to different parts of the body. For instance, beta-carotene—and other carotenoids—is particularly advantageous to eye health;

flavonoids to heart health; lycopene to prostate health; and pro-anthocyanin to urinary tract health.

Benefits of Antioxidants

There is a plethora of antioxidants present in various food ingredients that can be classified into various categories. They can be divided on the basis of solubility—water-soluble and fat-soluble; source—natural antioxidants and synthetic antioxidants; and action mechanism in our body . . . but it is rather complex for the layman to understand. We will be focussing on natural antioxidants, especially non-enzymatic antioxidants, as they are more closely associated with nutrition.

Natural antioxidants are either produced in the human body through metabolic processes or are supplemented from other natural sources. They are further classified as enzymatic and non-enzymatic antioxidants. Enzymatic antioxidants, aka endogenous antioxidants, are those produced in the human body and non-enzymatic antioxidants, aka exogenous antioxidants, are those that are not found in the human body.

Antioxidants are known for:

- Slowing ageing
- Decreasing cancer risk
- Increasing lifespan
- Detoxifying body
- Helping the skin glow
- Improving mood disorders
- Improving memory
- Building immunity
- Decreasing the chances of age-related blindness

Endogenous Antioxidants

Certain antioxidants are produced inside the body and are referred as endogenous antioxidants. In simple terms, endogenous antioxidants are made by our bodies and cannot be obtained from food sources. Most importantly, endogenous antioxidants are more powerful than those that are obtained from food. They are capable of repairing all free-radical damages by initiating cell regeneration. As an individual gets older, the body's production of endogenous antioxidants declines simultaneously. Due to this decrease in endogenous antioxidants, one experiences premature ageing and degenerative diseases like diabetes, Alzheimer's, cancer, heart disease, etc. On the other hand, the higher levels of these antioxidants prevent age-related health issues.

1. ***Glutathione:*** Considered the master antioxidant, it is the most powerful antioxidant found in every single cell of our body. It has the unique character of maximising the performance effect of other antioxidants like vitamin C, vitamin E, alpha-lipoic acid (ALA), etc. Its primary function is to protect cells and prevent peroxidative damage. It also helps in detoxification, energy utilisation, and preventing diseases associated with ageing. It helps in eliminating toxins from the cells and protects from the harmful effects of radiation, chemicals, and environmental pollutants. As we age, the property of producing glutathione decreases. Consuming high-quality whey protein, curcumin, raw dairy products, eggs, and grass-fed animal meat helps in promoting the production of glutathione.

2. ***Alpha-lipoic acid (ALA):*** Considered as the universal antioxidant, it is basically a fatty acid produced by the body itself, which is also a powerful antioxidant which helps in eradicating free radicals. It is also quite beneficial for people with brain diseases, like Alzheimer's, as this antioxidant can easily be transported to one's brain. It also plays a significant role in energy production and maintaining proper metabolism. It has unique characteristic of regenerating the already-used antioxidants like vitamin C, vitamin E, and glutathione in the body.

3. ***Coenzyme Q10 (CoQ-10 or Ubiquinone):*** It is a lipid-like substance that is considered an antioxidant, which is produced naturally in our body. It is mostly found in organs like heart, kidneys, and liver. It is necessary for the health of body tissues. It prevents and/or treats cardiovascular diseases, high blood pressure, AIDS, ageing, and kidney failure.

Exogenous Antioxidants

The antioxidants that are supplied from the food or that comes from outside the body are exogenous antioxidants. These antioxidants are obtained from the diet. Vitamin C, vitamin A, and vitamin E are some of the few examples of exogenous antioxidants. Exogenous antioxidants are only capable of stimulating cell regeneration, but are not capable of initiating cell regeneration like endogenous antioxidants. Hence, they are considered less powerful than endogenous antioxidants. Nowadays, supplements of exogenous antioxidants are readily available in the market as it is impossible to obtain all the desired exogenous antioxidants solely from the diet.

Exogenous Antioxidants—Their Sources and Uses

Antioxidants	**Sources**	**Remarks**
Allium sulphur compounds	Leeks, Onions, garlic, shallots	It has anti-inflammatory properties, lowers cholesterol levels, controls blood pressure, helps in detoxification, decreases blood clots, and is beneficial for healthy heart.
Anthocyanins	Eggplant, grapes, berries, pomegranate, tomatoes, currants; red to purplish blue-coloured leafy vegetables, grains, roots, and tubers.	Extensively useful as it has anti-cancer properties, anti-diabetic effects, anti-obesity effects, antimicrobial properties. It is also effective in visual health.
Astaxanthin	It is the red pigment identified in crustaceans (shellfish), salmon flesh/ roe. Found in marine animals.	It helps in anti-ageing HDL (good cholesterol) and decreasing oxidation of LDL (bad cholesterol); thereby lowering the risk of heart diseases. Also protects eyes from blindness and cataract, and the brain from dementia and Alzheimer's.

contd ...

Antioxidants	Sources	Remarks
Beta-carotene	Brightly coloured fruits and vegetables such pumpkin, carrots, apricots, peas, spinach, kale, mangoes, parsley, lettuce, squash, sweet potatoes, etc.	Promotes good skin health by reducing sun sensitivity. It protects against lung cancer and reduces macular degeneration. It prevents free-radical damage.
Catechins	Red wine, tea, beer, cacao liquor, chocolate, cocoa, etc.	Helpful in heart diseases and strokes. It lowers LDL cholesterol, fights ovarian and breast cancers, and even Alzheimer's disease.
Copper	Seafood, oysters, lean meat, milk, nuts, legumes, dark chocolate, etc.	Key role in making red blood cells, improves immune system and maintains nerve cells, helps in absorption of iron. Its deficiency may lead to cardiovascular disease and osteoporosis. It also helps in formation of collagen and elastin, which are two major components of structural bodies.

Antioxidants	Sources	Remarks
Cryptoxanthin	Red peppers, pumpkin, mangoes, orange rind, butter, apples papaya, etc.	It helps in fighting free-radical damage to cells and stimulates repair. It is a precursor to vitamin A.
Flavonoids	Tea, green tea, red wine, citrus fruits, onion, apples, soy products, pomegranate, chocolate.	Reduces risk of cancer, asthma, stroke, etc. It also has anthistamine, and mood-changing characteristics.
Gingerol	Ginger	It has anti-cancer properties, it restricts ageing, boosts immune system, aids in digestion, and treats nausea.
Indoles	Cruciferous vegetables such as broccoli, cabbage, cauliflower, Brussels sprouts, kale, radish, turnip, etc.	Helps prevent prostate cancer, breast cancer, lung cancer, colon cancer, etc. It aids in getting rid of toxins and has anti-inflammatory properties as well.
Lignans	Flaxseeds, seasame seeds, brain, whole grains, vegetables.	Lignans balances hormone levels in the body. In men and women, it balances testosterone and oestrogen levels

Antioxidants	Sources	Remarks
		respectively. It is good for breast health, reduces LDL cholesterol levels, and decreases the risk of cardiovascular disease. It also helps in improving digestion and strengthens hair.
Lutein	Corn, green leafy greens (such as spinach), papaya and oranges.	Lutein plays a key role in protecting eyes from various diseases. One suffering from poor vision can improve it in low contrast conditions with the help of lutein.
Lycopene	Pink and red fruits and vegetables like tomatoes, pink grapefruit, watermelon, guava, papaya, sweet peppers, etc.	Protects body from stress and provides safety from environmental toxins and chronic diseases. It lowers the risk of cancer and maintains proper cholesterol levels. It also protects from sunburn.
Manganese	Seafood, lean meat, milk, nuts, seeds, and whole grains.	It helps in regulating blood sugar levels and helps in decreasing inflammation and pain as well. It also helps in maintaining good thyroid health.

Antioxidants	Sources	Remarks
Polyphenols	Thyme, oregano, cloves, cocoa powder, dark chocolate, berries, beans, nuts.	Protects from different kinds of cancers, cardiovascular diseases, osteoporosis, and diabetes.
Resveratrol	Red wine, blueberries, cocoa, grapes, and peanuts.	It is a powerful anti-inflammatory antioxidant beneficial for heart diseases and other conditions. It is helpful in decreasing the chances of prostate cancer and lowers blood pressure as well. It is also effective in preventing Alzheimer's disease.
Selenium	Rice, corn, wheat and other whole grains; Seafood, offal, lean red meat, chicken, nuts eggs, cheese and legumes. Vegetables grown in selenium rich soil.	Selenium is believed to help fight cell damage by oxygen-derived compounds and help protect against cancer.

Antioxidants	Sources	Remarks
Vitamin A	Dairy produce, eggs, and liver.	It helps in protecting from night blindness and reduces the risk of cancer. It supports bone health and boosts immunity.
Vitamin C	Citrus fruits and other fruits like cherries, kiwifruit, mangoes, papaya, strawberries, watermelon, tomatoes, etc. Vegetables like cabbage, broccoli, Brussels sprouts, spinach, mustard greens, cauliflower, etc.	It is required for growth, development and repair of all body tissues. It is also involved in formation of collagen, absorption of iron, and maintains cartilage, bones, and teeth strength.
Vitamin E	Sunflower and vegetable oils, nuts, almonds, avocados, seeds, whole grains, and green leafy vegetables.	It helps in preventing coronary heart disease inflammation. It promotes better eye health and lowers risk of cancer.

Antioxidants	Sources	Remarks
Zeaxanthin	Spinach, kale, lettuce, turnip, broccoli, zucchini, kiwifruit, raw carrot, etc.	It reduces the risk of chronic eyes diseases.
Zinc	Seafood, lean meat, milk, nuts.	It boosts the immune system, thereby promoting healthy growth during childhood. It also helps in healing wounds, improving memory, and treating cold.
Zoochemicals	Red meat, offal, fish, dairy products.	It reduces risk of blood clotting and inflammation. It is good for eye health, prevents, cancer, improves brain functions, and boosts the immune system.

Classification of Antioxidants

Antioxidants can be easily understood by classifying them on the basis of their nature and the character they exhibit:

1. ***Antioxidant vitamins:*** These are those vitamins that display the characteristics of antioxidants as well. Examples: vitamin A, vitamin C, and vitamin E.

2. ***Antioxidant minerals:*** These are those minerals that display the characteristics of antioxidants as well. Examples: Copper, iodide, manganese, and zinc.
3. ***Antioxidant protein:*** Are those proteins which display the characteristics of antioxidants as well. Examples: Alpha-lipoic acid and glutathione.
4. ***Antioxidant enzymes:*** Are those enzymes and coenzymes which display the characteristics of antioxidants as well. Examples: DHEA, (dehydroepiandrosterone) and catalase.
5. ***Antioxidant phytonutrients/phytochemicals:*** Phytochemicals are those chemicals that are present in plants and give them their colour and smell. They are also known as phytonutrients. Examples: Carotenoids, flavonoids, and resveratrol.
6. ***Antioxidant hormones:*** Certain hormones display antioxidant characteristics. Example: Melatonin.

Thus, in the system where harmful free radicals exist, there is also the presence of its antidote, which are the highly beneficial antioxidants. Undoubtedly, antioxidants are tremendously beneficial for human health, and it is our duty to incorporate as much variety of them as possible in our diet to derive maximum benefits. Each antioxidant has a distinct characteristic and purpose; hence, a broader incorporation of antioxidants will be more meaningful and appropriate in one's healthy life.

3
Prebiotics and Probiotics

'Almost all our health concerns can be traced back to our belly. Ensure a healthy gut and the rest will take care of itself.'
—Behzad Azargoshasb

Biotic is a term that is associated with something or resulting from living things, especially in their ecological relations. Two words are prominent in this context for being beneficial to the human diet when they are prefixed with 'pre' and 'pro' to constitute terms—prebiotics and probiotics. Both the terms are gaining utmost popularity as they are penetrating into the lives of the ones who are conscious about their diet and health.

Sounding almost the same, the basic difference needs to be understood in broader aspect and what purpose they serve in the well-being of humankind.

Prebiotics

Prebiotics are a special kind of plant fibre that is non-digestible and is consumed by humans to feed and nourish the good bacteria already present in the large bowel— large intestine. It acts and performs as a fertiliser for the good bacteria present in the gut; thereby improving the quantity of good bacteria as compared to bad bacteria. The increase in good bacteria culture has been significantly proved to be associated with the overall well-being—from one's stomach to their brain.

Prebiotic fibres are found in numerous fruits and vegetables like the skin of apples, bananas, onions, leeks, asparagus, chicory roots, beans, garlic, barley, flaxseeds, and oats. All these food ingredients have very minute amount of prebiotic fibre except chicory roots. Chicory root contains the highest amount of prebiotic fibre. Nowadays, prebiotic fibre supplements are available in the local markets. They are mild in texture and somewhat tasteless. Prebiotics are unaffected by cold, heat, acid, or time; hence, no extra precaution is required to increase their efficiency in the gut.

In recent years, it has been researched that the colon plays an important role in the well-being of an individual. The healthy bacteria in the bowel functions to strengthen the bowel wall along with improving mineral absorption and aiding in the regulation of hormone production, thereby executing varied essential beneficial functions. Prebiotics generally fertilise the good bacteria and restrains the growth of bad or disease-causing bacteria.

If one doesn't include prebiotic fibre in their diet, the good bacteria start starving, and over a period of time, gradually dies. The death of good bacteria leads to an increase in bad or unhealthy bacteria. It needs to be understood that prebiotics are not digested by humans, instead they themselves are digested by bacteria in the gut. In fact, prebiotics pass through the small intestine without being digested and is fermented when it reaches the large intestine.

Some examples of prebiotics include fructo-oligosaccharides, galacto-oligosaccharides, arabinose, galactose, inulin, raffinose, mannose, lactulose, stachyose, mannan-oligosaccharides, xylo-oligosaccharides, palatinose, lactosucrose, glycol-oligosaccharides, isomalto-oligosaccharides, soybean oligosaccharides, etc.

The consumption of prebiotics gives a feeling of being full to the individual and this sense of satiety is beneficial to those who are struggling to lose weight or trying to maintain a healthy weight.

Benefits of Prebiotics

- Improves the immune system
- Helps in calcium absorption and bone density
- Maintains weight
- Improves the growth of good bacteria
- Controls bad bacteria and a leaky gut
- Controls metabolism
- Aids in chronic digestive disorders
- Helps in inflammatory bowel movement
- Provides relief from poor digestion of lactose

Thus, in simple words, an abundance of good and beneficial bacteria leads to great health from physical, mental, and emotional perspectives; and prebiotics are, undoubtedly, the best at performing this task.

Probiotics

Probiotics are the live bacteria and yeasts that are found in yogurt (curd) and other dairy products. It is generally recommended by doctors to those who are on the dose of antibiotics in order to reduce the gastrointestinal side effects of medications.

It is found in yogurt, which is made from milk fermented by friendly bacteria like lactic acid and bifidobacterial;

buttermilk, certain cheeses with live bacteria; kefir, fermented probiotic milk drink with kefir grain culture; sauerkraut, finely shredded cabbage fermented with lactic acid bacteria; tempeh, fermented soybean product; kimchi, fermented cabbage; kombucha, fermented tea drink; gherkins, pickled cucumber; etc.

What needs to be understood here is that just anyone doesn't know which good bacteria would benefit them. Moreover, consuming probiotic is just a hopeful assumption that certain bacteria would prove to be beneficial. Our body comprises of two kinds of bacteria—good bacteria and bad bacteria. Probiotics are all about good bacteria like lactobacillus and bifidobacterium. They promote health and are effective in the functioning of the body by fighting the bad bacteria. Probiotics also comprise good yeast like *Saccharomyces boulardii*, which also contributes in promoting health.

Probiotics are helpful when they are alive, and they may die due to heat, stomach acid, or with the passage of time. What kinds of health benefits are provided by them still pose a huge dilemma. But various probiotic species are helpful in treating childhood diarrhoea, irritable bowel syndrome (IBS), and several other bowel infections. Probiotics also prevent the growth of pathogens by synthesising antimicrobial compounds.

It has been found that probiotics get destroyed by stomach acid and digestive enzymes. So, it is better to have them with the kinds of food that act as a buffer against stomach acid and digestive enzymes, thereby protecting probiotics. As the digestion process speeds up during and after meals, probiotics can be consumed with meals to create a more suitable environment for them.

Benefits of Probiotics

- Improves digestive health
- Reduces risk of antibiotic-related diarrhoea
- Improves mental health
- Provides relief from stomach and gastrointestinal disorders
- Reduces the need of antibiotics
- Inhibits diseases caused by rotaviruses in infants
- Supports the synthesis of nutrients and augments the immune system expanding intestinal tract health
- Decreases the chances of allergies in vulnerable people
- Controls hypertension
- Keeps a check on one's cholesterol levels

Thus, undoubtedly, probiotics are packed with numerous benefits and are a great combination with prebiotics. In simple terms, prebiotics feed the probiotics and both work simultaneously to enhance the digestive system, which leads to a boost in an individual's overall health. Metaphorically, probiotic living organisms are the seeds that feed upon the prebiotic fibre, acting as fertiliser and water, leading the seed to flourish and grow.

4

Detoxification—A Boon

'Let go of toxic control, in order to regain healthy control.'

—Kayla Rose Kotecki

Our modern lifestyle has exposed us to several things that are not favourable for our health, and in some ways, have prohibited us from maintaining a healthy lifestyle. This lifestyle has led us to the habit of consuming processed foods—canned foods, packaged food, frozen foods, etc.—non-organic produce—foods that are exposed to dangerous pesticides and germicides—using certain personal care products like shampoos, lotions, and cosmetic products that have a huge amount of harmful ingredients like parabens, formaldehyde, etc., which are responsible for cementing harmful particles in our body. Even the environmental conditions like pollution, smoking, and consumption of various medicines also amount to the build-up of toxins in our body. This whole process cements toxic substances in our body. But what exactly are toxic substances or toxins and how do we deal with them?

A toxin can be simply stated as any harmful substance that has some or the other negative impact on our health. Toxins can be poisons, chemicals, pollutants, synthetic food ingredients, pesticides, etc., which cause harm to the body. Toxins are present in the air we breathe, the water we drink, and the food we consume. Everyone is in regular contact with pollutants, i.e. toxins. Toxins keep on accumulating in our body, resulting in various health issues during our lifetime.

Some of the examples of toxins are:

- Antinutrients—Alcohol, processed foods, trans-fats, caffeine, etc.
- Internal metabolic toxins—Bile, urea, free radicals, stool, carbon dioxide, nitrogen, etc.
- Chemicals—Pesticides, cleaning products, glue, etc.
- Infectious organisms—Bacteria, yeast, viruses, etc.
- Unhealthy conditions—Excess or improper or frequent medications
- Stress—Financial strain, work pressure, anxiety, tiredness, etc.
- Unhealthy mental phase—Overeating, destructive mental patterns, addictions, etc.
- Ambient distractions—Comprehensive noise, smells, light, etc.
- Overstimulation—Television, computers, smart-phones, etc.
- Isolation—From spirituality, social connection, and/or nature, etc
- Negative mindset—Fear, anger, guilt, etc.

What Is Detoxification?

Detoxification is a process to remove toxins from the body. In other words, removal of waste and harmful substances from the body and cleansing is referred to as detoxification or detox.

Every human body is capable enough to remove toxins from it naturally. It has certain systems in place to remove waste from within. There are five organs that play a crucial role in this matter:

- **Skin:** Toxins are removed along with sweat
- **Liver:** Its primary job is to filter and excrete waste, hormones, drugs, and foreign substances
- **Lungs:** It removes carbon dioxide during the process of breathing
- **Large intestine:** Transforms waste into stool and expels it through defecation
- **Kidneys:** Filters blood and removes waste from body through urination

Thus, our body is continuously detoxifying and cleansing the system. The process of detoxification can be carried out in numerous ways and several processes contribute to it, which leads to the removal of toxins.

Ways to Detoxify

Detoxification should be considered an important part of one's lifestyle as it cleanses, nourishes, and recharges the body. There are various processes by which the human body can remove toxins and this is quite crucial for improving one's health. By incorporating the measures given below, the benefits of detoxification can be reaped to fullest:

1. ***Reduce the consumption of alcohol:*** Almost 90 per cent of alcohol consumed by an individual is metabolised by liver enzymes, converting it into a toxin called acetaldehyde (cancer-causing chemical). Acetaldehyde is converted into acetate, a harmless substance, only by the liver. The

excessive consumption of alcohol is harmful for the liver as it leads to fatty liver—fat accumulation around liver—and this doesn't allow the liver to function properly and remove harmful toxins effectively. Hence, alcohol consumption should be controlled for proper toxin removal.

2. ***Proper and quality sleep:*** Sleep is another pivotal aspect for maintaining a healthy body, and one must ensure that she/he sleeps adequately. Sufficient sleep of 7 to 8 hours permits brain to recharge itself and remove toxins as well. With improper sleep, toxins like beta-amyloid build up in the body and create several issues like Alzheimer's. It may also lead to anxiety, stress, heart diseases, obesity, high-blood pressure, and so on.
3. ***Adequate water consumption:*** Apart from quenching thirst, regulating body temperature, aiding digestion, lubricating joints, and helping in nutrient absorption, water also detoxifies the body by removing toxins through urination, breathing, or sweating. If such toxins are not removed, they build up in the bloodstream, causing harm to the entire body. The toxins are capable of threatening various bodily functions like restricting the production of haemoglobin, damaging the enzymes, reducing the body's capacity to fight the damage caused by free radicals, thereby resulting in premature aging. It even results in weaker bone density as it displaces the structural minerals from our body.
4. ***Drinking water in the morning:*** Drinking lukewarm water after waking up is also a good way to detoxify. Consuming lukewarm water or lemon water in the morning on an empty stomach aids in kick-starting

the day and ushering the toxins out of the body. It increases metabolism and improves digestion.

5. ***Fasting:*** Fasting means abstaining from consuming food for a day, which is also an effective means of detoxifying the body. One has to remain on a liquid diet as this allows the digestive system to rest and rejuvenate. In doing so, the entire body resets, recovers, and rejuvenates which helps the body function with great efficiency.
6. ***Refraining from bad habits:*** People these days are generally trapped in the clutches of bad habits like smoking, drinking alcohol, or consuming caffeine. Such habits introduce toxins in the body, so refraining from such habits is also a means of detoxification. If one is used to these habits, it is impossible to quit in a single day, but the trick is to keep reducing the intake gradually.
7. ***Reducing consumption of sugar and processed foods:*** The consumption of sugar and processed foods lead to obesity and chronic diseases like heart problems, cancer, and diabetes. Such diseases hamper the natural detoxification process of the body. Hence, it is better to avoid junk food and keep our body's detoxification system healthy.
8. ***Consuming antioxidant-rich foods:*** As mentioned in the previous chapters, free radicals harm our body's cells. The antioxidants deactivate the harmful effects of free radicals and protect our body from toxins as well. So, having an antioxidant-rich diet is recommended.
9. ***Organic foods:*** One should rely on organic food as much as possible as they are free from harmful pesticides, insecticides, germicides, preservatives, and

other chemicals. Its consumption makes us free from toxins. So, it can be said that consumption of organic food eliminates the formation of potential toxins in the body.

10. ***Prebiotic foods:*** Detoxification system remains strong if the gut is healthy as intestinal cells perform the detoxification process. Gut health is related to prebiotics— specialised non-digestible fibre—that feed probiotics. Consumption of antibiotics disturbs the gut health and weakens the immune system. Foods like onion, garlic, tomatoes, bananas, oats, etc., are some of the foods to be consumed as prebiotics.

11. ***Reduce salt intake:*** Salt consumption helps in retaining water in the body. The removal of water from the body helps in removing toxins, hence, the water consumption can be increased and salt consumption can be reduced. In fact, the potassium-rich foods like potatoes, squash, kidney beans, bananas, spinach, etc., counterbalance the harmful effects of excess sodium.

12. ***Workout:*** Exercising regularly has many benefits as it ensures a longer and healthier life. It also reduces the risk of many chronic diseases. It helps reduce inflammation, which, in turn, improves the detoxification system so that the body can work efficiently to protect us from various diseases. In fact, massaging also puts pressure on certain points of the body and helps in getting rid of stress. The typical points where the toxins build up are massaged, which result in detoxification.

13. ***Meditate:*** Stress is one of the main culprits of toxins in our body, so it needs to be controlled and managed. Meditation is an effective tool to manage stress and detoxify our body. Meditation needs to be understood and prioritised in our daily wellness.

Thus, detoxification strategies and adapting techniques can be different, but all leads to the wellness of humankind. All the methods should be inculcated as a habit in our lifestyle and only then can we experience the genuine advantages of the detoxification system. Detoxification gifts better lifestyle and health to an individual; it is a boon to our body; hence, it should be practised without fail.

5
Weight Management

'If you keep good food in your fridge, you will eat good food.'
—Errick McAdams

People have been adapting to new lifestyle changes at such speed and ease that several new issues have surfaced over the last couple of decades. The changes in one's lifestyle include creating comfort zone around oneself regarding physical activities, not exercising, and eating junk food—all of which have disastrous results on one's health. This, in turn, leads to mental distress. Hence, these lifestyle changes have become a threat to the balance of our physical as well as mental health. This has also given birth to a complex disease known as obesity.

Obesity is not a cosmetic concern; it has opened doors to several other diseases like diabetes, heart diseases, high blood pressure, and certain cancers. People suffering from obesity are advised by their doctors to shed extra kilos to maintain a long and healthy life. Apart from working out, there are numerous dietary habits people who want to lose weight can choose from. In this chapter, we are going to talk about the different diets along with their pros and cons.

Ketogenic Diet

Ketogenic diet, also known as Keto, is a diet plan that emphasises on the consumption of low-carbohydrate, high-fat, and moderate protein. The philosophy which works in Keto diet is that when an individual reduces the carb intake, their body starts consuming fat and protein as its fuel requirement; this process is known as ketosis. During ketosis, the ketones—molecules produced in liver from fat—are used by the body as fuel source because glucose (carb) is limited. Thus, while on a keto diet, the body enters in the phase of ketosis where the fat starts burning, leading to weight loss.

During this diet, the consumption of carbohydrate should not exceed 50 gm—it can remain between 20–50 gm—per day. Generally, more calories are required to transform fat into energy as compared to carbohydrate, and this, perhaps, may be the reason for weight loss. This diet is not a long-term process for health benefits, but its main intention is to lose weight. Apart from losing weight, it is considered to be beneficial for people who suffer from heart diseases, epilepsy, and acne.

Keto has certain side effects as well. Those who are on this diet may face constipation, mild low blood sugar (hypoglycaemia), decreased bone mineral density, and deficiency of certain vitamins and mineral. It can even lead to kidney stones or high level of acids in the body (acidosis), but this condition is quite rare.

Nutrient Intake for Energy Needs

- Carbohydrate—5 per cent
- Fat—75 per cent
- Protein—20 per cent

Another interesting aspect of the keto diet is that it increases the sense of satiety and reduces hunger, which is one of the reasons for weight loss.

People with following disorders or complications should avoid going on the keto diet:

- Type 1 diabetes
- Eating disorders
- Those who have had cholecystectomy
- Thyroid
- Multiple Sclerosis

Benefits of the Keto Diet

1. Normally, our body is in a habit of using glucose as a source of energy but the keto diet replaces glucose with ketones as fuel for the body to obtain energy. Thus, the body gets the ability to switch over it fuel source—between carb and fat—whenever required and even allows both to be used more efficiently.
2. Our body derives energy from ketones instead of glucose, and this helps in lowering the blood sugar levels. Thus, it lowers glucose levels and increases insulin sensitivity. The insulin sensitivity is of great importance as it prevents type 2 diabetes, obesity, and various other diseases.
3. On this regime, the body uses fat as fuel despite stored glycogen, resulting in fat loss. This, eventually, results in weight loss.
4. It improves the overall performance of the body and even safeguards it from diseases like Alzheimer's, Parkinson's, epilepsy, cancer, diabetes, etc.

5. The energy released from ketones are much more than the energy released from glucose, thereby improving one's stamina. It boosts the recovery of muscles, which in turn improves endurance and resistance training.
6. Ketones improve blood circulation and heart's functions. The blood flow and mechanical efficiency of the heart improves tremendously when it runs on ketones.

Disadvantages of the Keto Diet

1. Harvard T. H. Chan School of Public Health has indicated that the keto diet has increased the risk of kidney stones and osteoporosis. It has even increased the blood levels in the uric acid, which is a risk factor for gout.
2. Emphasising heavily on fat nutrients has led to the danger of other nutrient deficiencies.
3. It also leads to keto flu—a group of symptoms that include headache, fatigue, nausea, and weakness.
4. One may also feel dehydrated while on this diet; hence, it is essential to keep oneself hydrated.
5. This diet permits one to consume only restricted foods and prohibits them from consuming delicious foods like rice, fruits, ice cream, etc. It is quite difficult to stick to this diet for long.
6. As the fibre intake is reduced, it leads to issues associated with gut health and constipation as it disturbs the digestive system.

Keto Diet Compatible Foods

- Eggs, chicken, meat, pork, lamb, game meat, etc.
- Fatty fish and other seafood like mackerel, herring, shrimp, cod
- Full-fat dairy products like yoghurt, butter, and cream
- Full-fat cheese
- Nut butter like almond and peanut butter
- Nuts and seeds like almonds, walnuts, peanuts, flaxseeds, chia seeds, pumpkin seeds, etc.
- Fats like sesame oil, olive oil, coconut oil, nuts oil
- Non-starchy and low-carb vegetables like tomatoes, mushrooms, peppers, broccoli, eggplant, zucchini, cabbage
- Leafy vegetables like spinach, kale, collard, lettuce, etc.
- Low-sugar fruits like strawberries, lemon, lime, raspberries, coconut, etc.
- Condiments like salt, pepper, unsweetened ketchup, lemon juice, fresh herbs, and various spices
- Dark chocolate with 70 per cent cocoa solids and low sugar
- Beverages like water, unsweetened tea or coffee

Keto Diet Restricted Foods

- Various breads, cookies, doughnuts, muffins
- Sugar, ice cream, and sugary products
- Sweetened beverages like soda, juice, sports drink, sweetened tea and coffee;

- Pasta and Noodles
- Oils like soya bean oil, corn oil, etc.
- Grains like wheat, oats, cereals, etc.
- Starchy vegetables like potatoes, sweet potatoes, peas, pumpkin, corn, etc.
- Beans like black beans, kidney beans, etc.
- Lentils
- Fruits like citrus fruits, bananas, pineapple
- High-carb sauces like dipping sauce, white sauce, brown sauce
- Alcoholic beverages

Atkins Diet

Considered as one of the best-known diets, Atkins diet is based on the doctrine of low-carb, high fat, and moderate protein consumption, similar to the Keto diet. But unlike Keto, the Atkins diet is broken into four phases, which emphasise on the quantity of carb intake in each phase. With each phase, the intake of carb is also increased.

The Atkins diet is split into four different phases:

1. ***Induction phase:*** In this phase, the carb intake is kept under the 20–25 gm per day for the first 15 days. During this time, as much fat and protein is consumed along with leafy vegetables. This dietary plan sparks weight loss. It is generally continued till, at least, 7 kg is lost.

2. ***Balancing phase:*** Here, the carb intake is increased gradually from 25–50 gm per day. In this phase, more nuts and fruit are added in the diet along with low-

carb vegetables. It is continued till the time further 5 kg is lost.

3. ***Fine-tuning phase:*** Here, the carb intake is raised to 50–80 gm per day until weight loss slows down. It usually goes on for about one month.
4. ***Maintenance phase:*** Carbohydrate intake is increased till it doesn't increase one's weight; the intake is between 80–100 gm per day. Even at this stage, the carbohydrate consumption is less as compared to an individual's normal diet.

Note: *If an individual restricts herself/himself to Phase 1, then it is just the Keto diet plan. In Phase 1, the body enters into the ketosis stage leading to weight loss but with the increase in carbohydrate intake, the body comes out of ketosis. This Atkins diet is much flexible as it allows for wider variety of foods to be consumed during this diet plan.*

Nutrient Intake for Energy Needs

- Carbohydrates—5–10 per cent (The percentage of carbohydrate varies in all four phases)
- Fat—60-65 per cent
- Protein—30 per cent

Benefits of the Atkins Diet

1. It leads to weight loss and improves cardiovascular health.
2. As it is flexible and not that restrictive, it is easy to stick to this diet plan.

3. It reduces triglyceride levels and increases HDL (High Density Lipoprotein), also known as good cholesterol.

Disadvantages of the Atkins Diet

1. As the carbohydrate intake is increased gradually, the intensity of weight loss weakens and people start gaining weight when they enter phases 3 and 4.
2. It doesn't make the body habitual of metabolic flexibility. The body doesn't remain in ketosis stage for long, and the main fuel-providing nutrient remains the carbohydrate itself.

Atkins Diet Compatible foods

- Eggs, chicken, meat, pork, lamb, and game meat
- Fish and shellfish like herring, cod, shrimp, mackerel, lobster, and prawns
- Dairy products like yoghurt, butter and cream
- Nut butters like almond and peanut butter
- Full-fat cheese
- Nuts and seeds like almonds, walnuts, peanuts, flaxseeds, chia seeds, and pumpkin seeds.
- Fats like sesame oil, olive oil, coconut oil, and nuts oil
- Non-starchy and low-carb vegetables like tomatoes, mushrooms, peppers, broccoli, eggplant, zucchini, and cabbage
- Leafy vegetables like spinach, lettuce, and kale
- Low-sugar fruits like strawberries, lemon, lime, raspberries, and coconut

- Condiments like salt, pepper, unsweetened ketchup, lemon juice, fresh herbs, and spices
- Beverages like water, unsweetened tea or coffee

Atkins Diet Restricted Foods

- Various breads, cookies, doughnuts, croissant, and muffins
- Sugar, ice cream, and sugary products
- Sweetened beverages like soda, juice, sports drink, sweetened tea and coffee
- Pasta and noodles
- Oils like soya bean oil, corn oil, etc.
- Grains like wheat, oats, cereals, etc.
- Starchy vegetables like potatoes, sweet potatoes, peas, pumpkin, corn, etc.
- Beans like black beans, kidney beans, etc.
- Lentils
- Fruits like citrus fruits, bananas, and pineapple
- High-carb sauces like dipping sauce, white sauce, and brown sauce

Palaeolithic Diet

Palaeolithic diet, also known as Paleo diet, is a diet plan that emphasises on the consumption of whole and unprocessed foods. It can be said that Paleo diet is a dietary pattern that is based on the concept of what people use to eat in Palaeolithic age, i.e. around 2.5 million to 10,000 years ago. This diet can lead to significant weight loss while improving one's metabolism.

This diet advocates avoiding the consumption of preservatives, additives, artificial flavours, sweeteners, flavour enhancers, hidden sugars, artificial food colours, etc.

This diet pattern is strictly based on the principles of rich nutrient diet. It stresses on the intake of fresh, organic vegetables and other produce like organic meat, fish and shellfish, organic vegetables, fruits, and berries, healthy fats—especially saturated fats, and nuts and seeds.

It prohibits the consumption of grains, legumes, processed sugar, and most dairy products. But today, it is somewhat next to impossible to avoid dairy products, hence, kefir (sour-tasting drink made from cow's milk fermented with certain bacteria), full-fat natural yoghurt, aged cheese, and butter are allowed in this diet.

Those who experience acute hyperglycaemia (an excess of glucose in bloodstream) and low blood sugar—due to which they encounter an outburst of hunger along with irritability, fatigue and clouded mind—Paleo diet can provide some relief as the individual derives energy from the nutrients. This helps in satiating hunger and controls the drop in energy levels along with stabilising the blood sugar level.

Nutrient Intake for Energy Needs

- Carbohydrate—30 per cent
- Fat—40 per cent
- Protein—30 per cent

Benefits of the Paleo Diet

1. It is effective in weight loss
2. It allows muscle growth
3. It improves metabolism

4. It manages stress and improves the quality sleep
5. It aids in burning stored fat with the proper intake of vitamin D and Omega-3/ Omega-6 fatty acids
6. It promotes brighter skin and hair growth
7. It improves the immune system
8. It prevents heart diseases and cancer
9. It reduces allergies
10. It lowers triglycerides
11. It provides energy stability in the body, hence, making one feel highly active
12. It is helpful in inflammation and inflammatory pain

Disadvantages of the Paleo Diet

1. The permitted food groups to be consumed normally exceed the RDA recommended daily allowances
2. The individual with heart, kidney, liver or pancreatic diseases must be kept under medical supervision as it is low in carbs and may lead to health complications
3. It leads to the deficiency of calcium as dairy products are restricted, leading to disease like rickets, osteoporosis, and fractures
4. It leads to the deficiency of minerals like selenium, magnesium, and manganese as legumes are restricted
5. It eliminates whole grains, decreasing the fibre intake, which is not beneficial for gut health

Paleo Diet Compatible Foods

- Fruits and berries (low-sugar fruits): Melon, grapes, bananas, citrus fruits, peaches, plums, apples, blackberries, blueberries, and strawberries
- Vegetables (non-starchy and starchy tubers and root vegetables): Cauliflower, cabbage, spinach, sweet potatoes, broccoli
- Nuts and seeds (that which contains Omega-3 fatty acids): Almonds, cashew nuts, pistachios, chia seeds, flax seeds, walnuts, etc.
- Eggs
- Lean meat (mostly grass-fed animals or wild game)
- Fish and shellfish
- Oils from fruits and nuts such as olive oil or walnut oil; sesame oil, coconut oil, ghee, butter, etc.
- Spices and herbs
- Salt (good quality sea salt)
- Condiments: Mustard, Apple cider or balsamic vinegar, mayonnaise, gherkins, olives, etc.\

Paleo Diet Restricted Foods

- Grains: Wheat or anything that contains gluten
- Legumes: Beans like red kidney beans, black beans; lentils, chickpeas, peanuts, tofu, soy products, etc.
- Dairy products: Milk and low-dairy products
- Processed vegetable oil and fats
- Refined sugars and carbohydrates: Pasta, bread, white sugar, sugary syrups, and fruit juices, etc.

- Processed food
- Food that contains preservatives and additives
- Artificial sweeteners

Dukan Diet

Dukan Diet is a high-protein, low-carbohydrate weight loss diet, created by Dr Pierre Dukan. It doesn't dictate norms on fat. This diet plan states that in its first phase, the unlimited quantity of lean protein (protein without fat) can be consumed while avoiding fat and carbohydrate. This protein, when it breakdowns, produces less calorie as compared to fat and carbohydrate, which leads to weight loss, giving a feeling of satiety. This diet also helps in maintaining weight.

One important and interesting aspect, which makes it effective, is that the protein generates heat within the body as more energy is required to breakdown the protein for digestion. So, more calories are burnt by consuming protein as compared to carbohydrates. The fat is, thus, consumed from the body as it is used as a source of fuel, leading to weight loss.

The Dukan diet consists of four phases:

1. ***Attack Phase:*** This phase has the maximum impact on weight loss and that, too, in a short period. It acts as motivation for the dieters as they observe and experience weight loss, making them stick to this diet. It advocates the consumption of as much protein as possible without incorporating fat and carbohydrate. This phase is quite restrictive on protein elements.

   All types of lean meat, including beef, pork, lamb, and other red meat; chicken, fish, and shellfish; vegetarian proteins like tofu, tempeh (fermented soybeans product), seitan (wheat protein), etc.; fat-free dairy products are permitted. Fruits, vegetables, carbohydrates, sugar, alcohol, and fats are restricted.

2. ***Cruise Phase:*** The phase with the longest period, it aims at reducing just 1 kg in a couple of weeks. It concentrates on the intake of protein-vegetable consumption.

   In this phase, non-starchy vegetables are incorporated on alternate days along with lean protein. Non-starchy vegetables like leafy greens, root vegetables, mushrooms, onions, cabbage, peppers, broccoli, and cauliflower are allowed on alternate days.

3. ***Consolidation Phase:*** This phase allows one to consume any food—but with small amounts of high-calorie food. It forces one to stick to the pure-protein concept one day a week. Here, carbohydrates and fats are also incorporated within certain limitations.

4. ***Stabilisation Phase:*** This phase allows for great flexibility when it comes to choosing the food ingredients—similar to previous phase—but with certain rules that must be followed:

   i. Walking for 20 minutes a day without fail
   ii. One day should be strictly based on pure-protein consumption policy each week

People who have existing health issues like diabetes, kidney ailments, or heart diseases; and pregnant women should not go on this diet. The high-protein intake is difficult to digest if you have kidney problems, and as it is a fibre-less diet plan, its insulin regulation becomes difficult for diabetic people. It may also raise issues like constipation, bad breath, headache, etc.

Benefits of the Dukan Diet

1. It aids in effective weight loss in the initial stages, which motivates one to continue this diet plan till the end.
2. It reduces obesity-related diseases.
3. It doesn't restrict the quantity of food to be consumed; hence, one doesn't feel hungry while on this diet.

Disadvantages of the Dukan Diet

1. As it is a high-protein, low-carb diet, weight loss in the initial stages is just due to the loss of water weight from the body. In the later stages, one doesn't witness significant weight loss.
2. This diet focuses on the consumption of expensive food items; hence, it is an expensive way of losing weight.
3. It is highly restrictive in its framework of selecting food ingredients and creates boredom within a few days.
4. It has side effects like headache, constipation, fatigue, etc.

Dukan Diet Compatible Foods

- Eggs
- Lean meat: Chicken, meat, veal, beef, ham, etc.
- All kinds of fish and shellfish: Salmon, mackerel, cod, prawns, lobsters, trout, etc.

- Dairy products: Fat-free yoghurt, fat-free cottage cheese, and skimmed milk.
- Vegetables like peppers, asparagus, mushrooms, broccoli, etc.

Dukan Diet Restricted Foods

- Fat is strictly to be avoided
- Carbohydrate intake should be minimal

The 5:2 Diet

The 5:2 diet is also known as the fast diet as it emphasises on the strategy of intermittent fasting. In the diet, one must consume food normally for five days a week and then restrict the calorie intake to just 500–600 calories for the remaining two days of the week. The deficiency in calorie eventually leads to weight loss. The benefits of intermittent fasting have been clinically proven; hence, this diet is undoubtedly gaining popularity.

This diet plan doesn't focus on the list of foods to be consumed; in fact, it focuses on the timing of food consumption. It allows one to eat anything they find nutritious and healthy.

According to numerous medical researches, alternate-day fasting doesn't allow one to eat much and this helps in releasing a special peptide hormone (PYY), which makes one feel full and help them eat less, leading to weight loss. On the days of fasting, one must rely on fibrous foods (like carrots, etc.) as they give a feeling of satiety and doesn't let people feel irritated or exhausted because they are hungry or thinking about eating the entire day.

Benefits of the 5:2 Diet

1. It aids in effective weight loss
2. It improves body composition
3. It boosts metabolism
4. It leads to better brain health
5. It can be continued for a longer period
6. Fasting at regular intervals has its own benefits like better digestion, lower blood sugar level, reduced inflammation, etc.

Disadvantages of the 5:2 Diet

1. It is not recommended for people with type 1 diabetes and hypoglycaemia
2. It is not advisable for those who suffer from iron deficiency anaemia
3. Pregnant women should not go on this diet
4. It is tough to stick to this diet plan as fasting is not everyone's cup of tea
5. People on this diet may overeat due to extreme hunger the next day
6. One may encounter the possibility of feeling hungry, irritability, fatigue, mood swings, or difficulty falling asleep

5:2 Diet Compatible and Restricted Foods

This diet doesn't restrict anything, but to get better results, low calorie and nutritious foods are preferred. So, one can eat vegetables, fruits, fibre, healthy fats, and lean meat.

- Vegetables: Cauliflower, peppers, broccoli, squash, leafy vegetables, etc.
- Fruits: Citrus fruits like lemon, lime, oranges, etc.; Starchy fruits and berries
- High-fibre foods: Beans, lentils, sprouted grains, legumes, etc.
- Fats: Olive oil, fish oils rich in Omega-3 and Omega-6 fatty acids
- Lean protein: Protein without fat of chicken, eggs, fish, meat, lamb, etc.
- Beverages: Water, herbal teas, and unsweetened coffee

As for restrictions, it only prohibits from consuming too much sugar.

***

Several people these days are fighting obesity-related complications. Obesity has been on a rise in almost every age group, and poses severe health risks to human beings. In India, more than 5 per cent of the population suffer from this complex disease; thus, it needs to be addressed immediately.

If one gets active and action-oriented at the onset of this disease, it would be easier to combat this issue. Various above-mentioned diet plans came into existence gradually, but people tend to get perplexed as to which diet plan would suit them the best. Both Keto and Atkins diet are based on the concept of low-carb intake and are effective in their purpose and premise. The Dukan diet, Paleo diet, and the 5:2 diet are also quite effective in weight loss and add to an individual's long-term wellness.

All the diets should be strictly monitored and, in case, one faces any issue while on a particular diet plan, they should immediately seek medical advice. In fact, if you suffer from existing health issues, it's always a great idea to first consult your physician before going on a diet.

Moreover, all these diet plans are more effective when they are accompanied by proper exercises because it allows one to absorb the nutrients consumed more efficiently, delivering better results. One needs to mentally prepare before starting a diet plan as it takes a strong willpower to achieve desired weight-loss goals.

Once the results are achieved, it is essential to continuously monitor the diet and stick to it. In simple terms, all the diet plans are designed to achieve significant weight loss, and the key to maintain it is in the hands of the individual by eating healthy and exercising regularly. The pleasure of the tongue has to be killed for the desire of a healthy body.

6
Rainbow Diet Is the Way to Go

'I've always believed in a rainbow diet. As many colors and foods as you can eat, the better.'
—Christie Brinkley

The world of fruits and vegetables is colourful and attractive. Each colour has a distinct characteristic to fight diseases, and this is only possible with the presence of phytochemicals. Phytochemicals are responsible for the colour of a fruit or vegetable. The fruits and vegetables are categorised into five major colour groups—red, blue/purple, green, orange, and white. So much of varied colour in various fresh produce is appealing and hence they are also referred as 'Rainbow nutrients". Each colour pigment has its own list of benefits it has delivered to mankind.

Phytonutrients

Phytochemicals are natural chemical compounds that are found in plants; they are responsible for their colour. They offer a great bouquet of health benefits to the humankind. It not only protects us from degenerative diseases—disease characterised by the loss of functions in organs or tissues and is irreversible—but also acts as superhero antioxidants as well.

This term is often used interchangeably with phytochemicals. But 'nutrients' is a more positive term when compared with 'chemicals'.

Phyto is a prefix that means relating to plants and is derived from the Greek word *phuton*.

Phytochemicals are not necessary for our body as they do not perform any functions. In fact, their deficiency doesn't expose us to any specific diseases. So, how come they offer numerous health benefits? They may not prevent any diseases, but they aid in reversing certain disorders and diseases. It combats free radicals that damage our cells and act as antioxidants. When phytonutrients are consumed, they activate a series of enzymes that clean up the free radicals before they could harm the body. This is how phytonutrients work.

An interesting characteristic associated with phytochemicals is that they don't get destroyed by any of the processing techniques like cutting, chopping, grating, cooking, etc. According to some researches on the finer aspects of this chemical, it is quite apparent that there are thousands of phytonutrients present in plants. Many are known to us and many have yet to be discovered.

Food Colour	**Phytonutrients**	**Food sources**	**Health Benefits**
Blue/ Purple	Anthocyanins, Resveratol (Flavonoid)	**Fruits:** Blackberries, blueberries, blackcurrants, dried plums purple figs, purple grapes,	• Rich in antioxidants • Anti-ageing • Boosts immunity • Repairs damage done to the liver by alcohol

Food Colour	Phytonutrients	Food sources	Health Benefits
		plums, and raisins **Vegetables:** Beetroot, purple carrots, eggplant, purple peppers, potatoes (purple flesh) black beans, red cabbage, red onions, etc. **Beverages:** Red wine	• Contains anti-inflammatory and anti-carcinogenic properties • Reduces risk of cardiovascular diseases, obesity, and and diabetes • Improves urinary tract health
Green	Lutein, Indoles, Sulforaphane, Carotenoids, Isoflavones, Glucosinolates, and Isothiocyanates	**Fruits:** Avocados, green grapes, kiwifruit, limes, green pears, etc. **Vegetables:** Artichokes, arugula, asparagus, bok choy, broccoli, Brussels sprout, Chinese cabbage, green beans,	• Rich in antioxidants • Induce detoxification of carcinogens • Limits the growth of hormones associated with with cancer • Reduces the of certain cancers • Reduces the risk of certain cancers • Prevents tumour

Food Colour	**Phytonutrients**	**Food sources**	**Health Benefits**
		cabbage, celery, cucumber, kale, leafy greens, leeks, lettuce, okra, peas, green capsicum, green peppers, spinach, watercress, zucchini, etc. **Legumes:** Green split peas, green lentils, etc.	growth • Maintains eye health (reduces the risk of cataract and macular degeneration) • Increases the production of Red Blood Cells • Heal wounds • Regulates white blood cells and and cytokines (substances released by certain cells of the immune system that affect other cells) • Crucial for protein synthesis, muscle contraction, and relaxation
Red	Anthocyanins, Lycopene	**Fruits:** Red apples, blood oranges, cherries, cranberries, red grapes, red pears, pomegranates,	• Has antimicrobial properties • Reduces the risk of cancer (especially prostate cancer)

Food Colour	Phytonutrients	Food sources	Health Benefits
		raspberries, strawberries, watermelon, etc. **Vegetables:** Beetroot, red peppers, radicchio, red onions, red potatoes, tomatoes, etc. **Legumes:** Red Beans, Kidney Beans, etc.	• Beneficial for heart health • Reduces inflammation • Improves overall health • Prevents bacteria that attack cells • Improves memory functions
White/ Brown	Allicin, Lignans, Isothiocyanates, Isoflavones, Phytates, Anthoxanthins	**Fruits:** Bananas, brown pears, white peaches, etc. **Vegetables:** Cauliflower, garlic, ginger, kohlrabi, parsnips, mushrooms onions, potatoes, shallots, turnips, white corn, etc.	• It is known for antiviral and and antibacterial properties. • It lowers cholesterol and blood pressure • It reduces the chances of stomach cancer • It is required for healthy functioning of heart • It inhibits tumour growth

Food Colour	Phytonutrients	Food sources	Health Benefits
		Legumes: Soybeans, lentils Whole grain seeds and nuts: Barley rye, flaxeeds, dates, etc.	
Yellow/ Orange	Carotenoids, Bioflavonoids, Bera carotene, Alpha-carotene, Beta-cryptoxanthin	**Fruits:** Yellow apples, apricot, cantaloupe, yellow figs, grapefruit lemon, mangoes, oranges, papayas, peaches, pineapples, tangerines, yellow watermelon, etc. **Vegetables:** Yellow beets, carrots, yellow peppers, yellow potatoes, pumpkin, sweet corn, yellow tomatoes, etc.	• Integral for eye health • Boosts immunity • Reduces the risk of heart diseases • Prevents cancer (especially lungs, oesophagus, and stomach)

Ways to Include Phytonutrients in Your Diet

- Establish a habit of eating fruits and vegetables in each meal or snack. Don't stick to only a single-coloured fruit or vegetable
- Sprinkle few nuts or dried fruits on every possible dish
- Incorporate berries in your cereals and salads
- Use as much fresh herbs as possible
- Flavour dishes with fresh garlic, ginger, and onion, whenever possible
- Eat as much raw fruits and vegetables as possible. Cooking, at times, destroys certain nutrients
- Incorporate barley, beans, lentils, etc., while preparing soups and stews
- Explore new fruits and vegetables now and then; don't just stick to your preferences
- Super nutrient flaxseeds can be consumed in small quantities
- Include multicoloured foods in your diet
- Don't avoid a particular food colour

Zoochemicals

Just how phytonutrients are present in plants, zoochemicals are present in animals. Thus, zoochemicals are compounds that are derived from animals and are considered to be beneficial for the health of human beings. Few compounds can have the characteristics of both phytochemicals and zoochemicals simultaneously. For instance, carotenoids, lutein, and zeaxanthin. Carotenoids can be available in vegetables like cantaloupe, carrots, mangoes, etc., as well as in egg yolk.

Some of the examples of zoochemicals are:

- **Methionine:** Found in dairy products like milk, cheese, and whey
- **Lutein and zeaxanthin:** Found in eggs
- **Methionine and linoleic acid:** Found in meat products
- **Selenium, astaxanthin, copper, zinc, Omega-3:** Found in seafood or marine animals

Ways to Incorporate zoochemicals in Your Diet

- Dairy products like milk, cheese, whey, curd, buttermilk, etc.
- Eggs dishes
- Poultry and meat products
- Seafood

Benefits of Phytonutrients and Zoochemicals

1. Phytochemicals have the capability to build a stronger immune system against harmful viruses, bacteria, and disease-causing agents.
2. They block the formation of carcinogens (substance that promotes formation of cancer) in the body. They fight the ill effects of the free radicals and act as powerful antioxidants.
3. They are the biggest enemies of cancer as they slow down the growth of cancer cells, kill the damaged cells that may be precursors to cancer, and reduce inflammation. They help in regulating hormones like

oestrogen and insulin, which may be the reason for breast and colon cancer.

4. They prohibit DNA damage and repair the already-damaged DNA mechanisms.
5. They reduce the risk of cardiovascular diseases
6. Zoochemicals reduce inflammation and the risk of blood clotting. They are beneficial for eye health, improve brain functions, and boost the immune system. They also prevent certain cancers.

7

Ayurveda—The Science of Healing from Within

'A faulty fire leads to improper functioning of the tissues which in turn, creates Ama in the gastro-intestinal tract and leading to poor synthesis of tissues.'

—Charaka Ayurvedic

Ayurveda is a comprehensive approach that advocates the healthcare rules from the ancient Indian system. It is an assemblage of two words: *Ayus*, meaning life and *Veda*, meaning knowledge. It focuses on the fundamental and rudimentary principles of nature in order to maintain overall health of an individual in terms of body, mind, and spirit. It also emphasises on one's lifestyle with proper sense of reasoning and logic associated with food and health.

Ayurveda has witnessed distinguished scholars in the ancient times, and they have enlightened humankind with invaluable concepts about Ayurveda and holistic well-being. The Ayurvedic academicians have put forth their scholarly advices in document format known as *Samahitas*.

Ayurveda has envisaged about several finer aspects of health and well-being, but three among it are crucial—*Tridoshas* (biohumors), *Agni* (digestive fire), and *Ama* (toxicity). The overall health and the doctrine of Ayurveda revolve around these three aspects. In order to understand them better, it is mandatory to delve into the ideas of *Panchamahabhutas* (five elements) and Six *Rasas* (six tastes) as well. Here is how these elements boost the overall health of an individual.

Panchamahabhutas (Five Elements)

Ayurveda sternly advocates that the physical world has been made of basic five elements: *Akash* (space), *Agni*, (fire), *Vayu* (air), *Jal* (water), and *Prithvi* (earth).

Six Rasas (Six Tastes)

The Indian cuisine is gifted with large selection of foods offering six tastes. They are sweet (*madhura*), salty (*lavana*), sour (*amla*), pungent (*katu*), astringent (*kasaya*), and bitter (*tikta*). It is considered that the various tastes have an impact on biological humours (doshas), which may increase or decrease with the consumption of particular tastes. Excessive consumption of any one taste is detrimental to one's health, but all the tastes must be included in the diet.

1. ***Sweet taste:*** It provides strength and vitality to the tissues and is nourishing and harmonising to the mind. It comprises sweet-tasting products, but also has ghee, rice, and fruits in the group.
2. ***Salty taste:*** It improves digestion and aids in clearing obstructions in the channels of the body. It makes people sweat and its excessive consumption leads to wrinkles, hypertension, and greying of hair.
3. ***Sour taste:*** It ignites the digestive fires and releases enzymes essential for digestion. It comprises sour-tasting foods like lemon, tamarind, amla, etc.

4. ***Pungent taste:*** It improves metabolism, which, in turn, boosts digestion. It consists of food products like onion, garlic, and pepper.
5. ***Astringent taste:*** It is responsible for healing ulcers and wounds in the body. It also helps in absorbing water and drying the fat content. It comprises food products like potatoes, most green vegetables, betel-nuts, tea, and apples.
6. ***Bitter taste:*** Responsible for eliminating bacterial elements and purifying blood; it consists of bitter gourd, lemon rind, fenugreek, etc.

Tridoshas (Biohumors)

Of all the five elements, two elements combine to form the three doshas. Every individual has any one of the predominating doshas, which decides their body's constitution.

1. ***Vata:*** It is the combination of two elements—air and space—and is considered the principle of movement. It controls motions such as swallowing, breathing, muscle movements, bowel movements, and urination. When vata features are imbalanced, the above-mentioned movements are affected, leading to health issues such as nervous disorders, bone problems, etc.
2. ***Pitta:*** It is the combination of two elements—fire and water—and is characterised as the principle of transformation. It controls digestion, sensory perception, temperature maintenance, and metabolism. When imbalanced, it occurs in the form of skin problems, inflammation, and heart diseases.
3. ***Kapha:*** It is the combination of two elements—water and earth—and is characterised as the principle of

stability and structure. It forms the structure of the body—from skeleton, fatty molecules to various organs. When it is imbalanced, it is evident in the form of cough, asthma, diabetes, and obesity.

Doshas are governed and controlled by six tastes:

Doshas	Stimulating Taste	Calming Taste
Vata	Astringent, bitter, pungent	Sour, sweet, salty
Pitta	Pungent, sour, salty	Astringent, bitter, sweet
Kapha	Sour, sweet, salty	Astringent, bitter, pungent

Agni (Digestive Fire)

The core of Ayurveda is centrally governed on the teachings of the digestive system. A healthy person has an effective digestive system. It strongly highlights the digestive fire, also known as *Jatharagni* (jathar means stomach and agni means fire). So, in order to have an effective digestion system, the fire in the stomach has to be intense that can easily digest anything.

The digestive fire consists of thirteen distinct fires to form the entire digestive system. The Jatharagni functions from mouth to anus and monitors the entire gastrointestinal tract. It basically helps in digesting complex food particles by breaking it into simpler forms. The seven tissues of the body—skin, blood, muscle, bones, adipose tissue, nerve tissue, and reproductive tissues—release enzymes that help in transforming the unstable tissues to build stable ones in the body, thereby improving the digestive system.

Depending upon the people and their body's constitution, digestive fire system is of four types:

1. ***Vishamagni:*** It indicates irregular hunger and conditions such as variable appetite, bloating, indigestion, constipation, flatulence, etc. The sweet and pungent tasting foods are consumed to overcome this condition.
2. ***Mandagni:*** It is characterised by conditions such as loss of appetite, slow digestion, feeling of heaviness after a meal, lethargic bowels, craving for sweets, bulky stool, etc. The bitter and pungent tasting foods are consumed to combat this state.
3. ***Tikshagni:*** It is characterised by issues like intense hunger with weak digestion. Ailments like thirst, dry throat, loose stool, and a burning sensation in intestines also persist. Mild-sour flavoured food ingredients are consumed in this state.
4. ***Samagni:*** It is a state of balanced hunger with proper digestion. Foods with all six tastes are preferred here.

The digestive fire plays a pivotal role and is responsible for proper food absorption, concentration, metabolic activities, and overall alertness. It keeps the appetite in check and constantly monitors the overall health. It is an essential element required in the strengthening of the immune system. It also keeps an individual in a lively state of intelligence, exuberance, and activeness.

Certain rules must be followed to maintain proper Agni:

- There is no need to eat or drink, unless one feels hungry or thirsty
- If you're thirsty, don't eat; if hungry, don't drink
- Drink warm water throughout the day as it ignites Agni. Avoid drinking cold water

- Eat a heavy breakfast, moderate lunch, and light dinner
- Incorporate spices like fresh ginger, black pepper, turmeric, cumin, and fenugreek as they enhance digestion
- Abstain from eating processed and packaged foods
- Eat dinner before 8:30 p.m.
- Avoid eating between meals; one has to build up their hunger for the next meal
- Masticating the food particles is essential as digestion starts with proper chewing
- Eat fresh fruits and vegetables and consume herbal drinks
- Don't drink water during or after a meal. Drinking water cools down the Agni immediately. If thirsty, rinse your mouth with one or two sips of water
- Drink water at least 45 minutes prior to a meal and 60 minutes after a meal
- Don't eat stale foods; rather stick to freshly cooked meals

Ama (Toxins)

When the digestive fire is imbalanced, the root cause of all diseases comes into force, which is called Ama. Ama can be defined as the internal toxins building up in the body due to inappropriate metabolic functioning. When the food is not digested properly, the undigested food gathers in the bowels and starts stinking and gets sticky. This undesired stuff blocks the intestines, blood vessels, and capillaries. This material further turns into toxins and enters the bloodstream after some time. Such toxins block the functioning of various organs. This further culminates into deadly diseases such as cancer, weakening of the immune system, heart diseases, etc. To put it simply, Ama is the mother of all diseases.

In order to avoid the build-up of Ama in the body, one has to have a balanced diet. At times, people start consuming food that shouldn't be consumed with each other, which makes Agni ineffective. Ama can be recognised by many symptoms such as loss of appetite, coating of the tongue with whitish-yellow film, foul breath, sluggishness, loss of vitality, sexual debility, lack of concentration, mental confusion, abnormal and muted taste, depression, and heart palpitations.

Reasons behind the Build-up of Ama in the Body

- Overeating
- Eating incompatible foods
- Consuming heavy foods and fried foods
- Eating processed and sugary content
- Excessive eating of sweet, sour, or salty products
- Harmful lifestyle—improper sleep, stress, lethargic life, lack of exercise
- Irregular eating habits
- Sleeping immediately after having dinner

How Ama Can Be Tackled

- ***Incorporating Herbs:*** The food with bitter and astringent taste has the capability to combat Ama as bitter-tasting food dries and drains away the ama and pungent tasting food digests and eliminates it. Herbs ignite the digestive fire if taken before a meal.

- ***Exercise:*** Exercise warms the body. Sweating while working out makes the Ama loosen its grip on the tissues, which aids them in moving towards the digestive tract, facilitating their elimination. This can be achieved by a steam bath as well. Walking for a few minutes after each meal is another way of getting rid of Ama.
- ***Yoga:*** The vital breath is the basic essence of life, and it can be improved by *pranayam*. It focuses the inhaling and exhaling, which aids in removing the toxins from the body.
- ***Fasting:*** It is also one of the significant ways of removing Ama from your body. Fasting should be done depending upon the constitution of the body.
- ***Selecting a proper diet:*** Incompatible foods must not be consumed. Foods that mutually respect each other must be preferred over anything else. Foods with sweet, sour, or salty taste must be reduced or avoided to a great extent.

Ayurveda is undoubtedly the healing science and can be described as the reason behind one's longevity. In order to be disease-free, one must have a strong digestive fire, otherwise their life will be in the clutches of toxins produced due to an unbalanced and ineffective digestive fire.

8
Aphrodisiacs

'Power is the ultimate aphrodisiac.'
—Henry Kissinger

Aphrodisiac is a heavenly substance that increases sexual desire and pleasure and is available in the form of food, beverage, scent, or drug. Actually, all food-based aphrodisiacs pleasure the consumer twice—first during consumption and second after consumption. Both the feelings are divine.

This chapter highlights some of the foods that are frequently found bearing the characteristics—knowingly or unknowingly—of aphrodisiacs, adding spiciness to our life by gratifying the goddess of love, beauty, and sexuality—Aphrodite.

Difficult to believe, but as true as the sun, in the Middle Ages, the meals were prepared for the kings and their family in silver utensils. Moreover, their food was also served in silver plates, whereas dal, curries, and milk were boiled with a big piece of gold. This piece of gold used to get dissolved slightly, after which it was washed and reused in other preparation till it got smaller. This was done as both gold and silver were considered aphrodisiacs.

It has been proven in various studies that individuals with problems related to blood circulation are relieved on consuming certain foods as they relax the blood vessels and improve blood flow to the genitals. Foods like pumpkins, walnut, and beef have L-arginine, an amino acid, which is converted to nitric oxide in the body, thereby increasing the flow. Similarly, Omega-3 fatty acids found in salmon and avocado and quercetin found in apples, berries, grapes, garlic, and dark chocolate also improve the blood flow and acts as an aphrodisiac.

Some of the natural aphrodisiacs are mentioned below.

Chocolate

Chocolate, the symbol of sensuality, is loaded with phenylethylamine (amphetamine and methamphetamine) that sparkles the nervous system and triggers the release of endorphins, which in turn increase libido. It also produces dopamine, a neurochemical related to sexual pleasure. Flavonoids (antioxidants) and serotonin found in chocolates also facilitate sexual performance of an individual. Chocolate is sensuous in its appearance, configuration, taste, aroma, and its overall feeling of incomparable pleasure.

Note: *Chocolate is considered as 'empty nutrient' rather than a 'dense nutrient'.*

Honey

Honey is a symbol of procreation. This silky semi-liquid is packed with boron, which expedites the regulation of oestrogen (in women) and testosterone (in men) and imparts the energy to perform. It is also packed with vitamin B, which is required for testosterone production. Its consumption increases nitric oxide, which helps in arousal.

Avocado

Vitamin E, also known as 'Sex Vitamin', is found in

avocados. It aids in maintaining one's youthful vigour and stabilises energy levels while retaining the sex drive. It also acts as a great lubricant. Its Aztec word is *Ahuacatl*, which literally translates to testicle tree, and clearly depicts its relation to sexual desire.

Figs

An arousing stimulant—heavy laden with flavonoids, polyphenols, and antioxidants. Figs are historically associated with sex and sin as in the Biblical story of Adam and Eve, figs signify sexuality as its leaves were used to cover their naked bodies. It is an essential fruit for good reproductive health as it is rich in minerals like magnesium, vitamin E, and zinc.

Asparagus

An excellent source of vitamin E, like Avocado, it also executes aphrodisiac characteristics. It contains folate (vitamin B), which increases histamine—significant for sexual delight. Considered to influence circulation in genitourinary system (organs involved in reproduction), it leads to great sexual high.

Ginger

Renowned for its excellent scent, which acts an aphrodisiac, energises the circulatory system. It works magic in the erogenous zones (areas that are very sensitive to sexual stimulation). If it is consumed by one about to indulge in a sexual act, it would heighten their pleasure.

Saffron

Considered to be a mood enhancer, it is a natural antidepressant and works as a remedy for erectile function. Whereas in women, it boosts arousal and lubrication.

People drink this expensive spice with milk after dinner and before going to bed. Legend goes that the rich were known to bathe in saffron-infused water to attain a sense of heightened pleasure.

Strawberry

An infamous symbol of seduction, its shape speaks volume about its charisma. Flooded with vitamin C, it promotes healthy blood flow and the production of oestrogen. It also contains desired minerals like magnesium, potassium, and folate, which heighten desire. Enriched with antioxidants, it makes people feel as well as look young.

Truffle

This earthy fungus smells similar to male sweat (androsterone), which attracts women and has a huge reputation in the world of sexual charm. It has maintained this reputation since the Roman era.

Watermelon

Considered the lycopene king, it is enriched with certain enzymes that relax the blood circulation in the groin region. It is packed with citrulline, but the rind of the fruit has more of this amino acid than the flesh.

Banana

Bromelain, an enzyme, triggers testosterone production and its potassium and Vitamin B content heighten the energy drive, thereby making it a food aphrodisiac.

Fenugreek

Its seeds are used in boosting one's libido. It has a few compounds that are used by the body to make sex hormones such as testosterone and oestrogen. It also heightens sexual pleasure. Moreover, it also has anti-inflammatory characteristics.

Papaya

A boon to women, it has been proven to be great in promoting menstruation, producing breast milk, and increasing female libido. Papaya is estrogenic in nature, which means that it has compounds that act as oestrogen.

Pepper

The bright red colour of pepper makes it divine and a symbol of love. It contains capsaicin, which releases epinephrine (adrenaline)—the chemical responsible for increased heart rate as well as the release of endorphins, a feel-good factor. It warms up the individual, pumping blood to the heart significantly and circulating it with stimulation of nerve endings, increasing pleasure.

Some of the other aphrodisiacs are bananas, oysters, red ginseng, etc.

Aphrodisiacs are psychological in nature and more of their performance is based on positivity of psychology. It is the brain that monitors all aphrodisiacs; hence, it becomes the play between ears rather the play between legs.

9
Food Combinations

'Conventional eating habits violate all of the rules of food combining in the preceding chapters and, since the majority of people manage to live for at least a few years and to "enjoy" their aches and pains and their frequent "spells of sickness," few of them are willing to give any intelligent consideration to their eating habits.'

—Herbert M. Shelton

One's health is defined by one crucial factor, and that is none other than the power of digestion. Our stomach is a sensible organ and it should not be treated like garbage, where you feed it whatever you want and whenever you want. In other words, whatever is on plate should not be consumed without understanding the food's element, potency, or compatibility. One must not consume food just for the sake of it, but it is healthier to choose and eat food sensibly. Eating with sensibility and awareness empowers digestion, which keeps many chronic diseases and ailments at bay.

You will be surprised to know but there are certain foods that pair well together and some do not. This concept of food combinations appeared in the Ayurvedic medicine in mid-

1800s. This has provided a foundation to several modern diets.

In order to understand this concept of combining certain foods, we need to explore various compatible and incompatible foods for our overall health.

Compatible Foods—Foods at Harmony

Two foods are said to be compatible with each other when their components work in complete unison, or maintain synergy, to maximise the nutritive value, hence, enhancing the health benefits. When one nutrient complements the other, it help in deriving the maximum benefits from the food you are consuming. Both the compatible foods work towards making your plate highly nutritious and beneficial.

Such synergy of food may exist within the same food groups or in different groups.

1. ***Onion and grapes:*** Onion has a large amount of quercetin, a powerful antioxidant. It has many beneficial values that help in providing relief from certain allergies and improves blood circulation, leading to better cardiovascular health. On the other hand, grapes are enriched with catechin, a polyphenol antioxidant, which helps in preventing cancer and cardiovascular diseases. Moreover, it also helps in losing weight. When consumed together, onion and grapes help in improving overall heart health and prevent blood clotting. Both the ingredients can be added in various salads.
2. ***Tomato and oil:*** Tomatoes consists of lycopene, an antioxidant that is helpful in preventing heart diseases and several cancers—especially lung, bladder, prostate, and breast. Generally, lycopene is not that easily

absorbed by the body when tomatoes are eaten raw. So, it is advised to cook tomatoes in oil. Extra virgin olive oil can also be added on the top, if the dish permits, as extra virgin olive oil should not be cooked. Thus, the combination of tomatoes and oil allow the tomatoes to provide maximum lycopene to the body.

3. ***Fish and garlic:*** The most beneficial Omega-3 fatty acids are the chief components of seafood. Fish is also rich in selenium and vitamin D—high in digestible protein and low in saturated fats. These components of fish help lower blood pressure and maintain proper heart rate. It also improves the functioning of blood vessels and reduces inflammation. When fish is cooked with garlic, its beneficial qualities are multiplied. It has been proven clinically that when eaten together, garlic and fish lower the LDL (Low Density Lipoprotein) cholesterol and harmful triglycerides, thereby leading to great heart health.

4. ***Spinach (leafy greens) and lemon:*** The iron in spinach is available in two forms:

    - Heme-iron: From animal sources like red meat, poultry, seafood, etc.
    - Non-heme iron: From plant sources like green leafy vegetables, nuts, grains, molasses, dried fruits, etc.

The iron we consume from non-heme (especially leafy vegetables) sources are not fully absorbed by the body. The ascorbic acid (vitamin C) facilitates the non-heme iron to be absorbed by the body easily. Hence, adding a few dashes of lemon juice to the preparation of leafy vegetables not only provide great taste but immense nutritive value as well.

Other iron-rich foods like beans, lentils, and chickpeas also does wonder with slight addition of lemon juice on it, as the absorption of iron is increased by the body.

5. ***Tomato and broccoli:*** Tomatoes are packed with antioxidants like lycopene, vitamin A, and vitamin C, whereas Broccoli is full of phytochemicals like beta-carotene, indoles, and isothiocyanates. When these two foods are eaten together, they help in combating cancer, especially prostate cancer. So, feel free to combine both foods to derive maximum health benefits.
6. ***Eggs and cheese:*** The egg is loaded with vitamin D and cheese, being the dairy product, has plenty of calcium in it. The body doesn't absorb calcium properly if it is not paired with vitamin D. So, in order to absorb the calcium thoroughly, cheese omelette is one of the options to include in your diet. It also keeps the bones strong and healthy.
7. ***Salad greens and almond/avocado:*** Salad greens have plant pigments like alpha-carotene, beta-carotene, and lutein. The salad greens help in reducing the risk of cardiovascular diseases, cataract, and certain forms of cancer. The MUFA (mono-unsaturated fatty acids) present in almonds or avocados helps in absorbing the nutrients of the greens more effectively. This food combination works towards lowering the LDL cholesterol more efficiently and allows the body to absorb all plant pigments compared to when the salad greens are consumed alone.
8. ***Rosemary and red meat:*** Rosemary is a herb that has antioxidants and rosmarinic acid. When red

meat is roasted, it releases harmful cancer-causing compounds—heterocyclic amines (HCAs)—due to a high cooking temperature. The rosmarinic acid in rosemary has been known to neutralise the HCAs. Thus, adding rosemary in the roasted preparation of lamb or beef makes your food healthier and dilutes the harmful effects of the HCAs. It is believed that the addition of rosemary can reduce the production of HCAs up to 88 per cent.

9. ***Brown rice and red kidney beans:*** Red kidney beans comprises of protein, fibre, vitamin B12, and minerals like magnesium and potassium. It helps in combating certain cancers—especially colon cancer—and heart diseases, along with controlling blood cholesterol and sugar levels. Brown rice contains ample magnesium and fibre. When both the food ingredients are consumed together, they complement each other and transform incomplete protein into complete protein. Complete protein has all the nine essential amino acids, which can't be produced by the human body and needs to be taken from an outside source.

10. ***Yogurt and almonds:*** A cup of yoghurt provides the body with the daily requirement of vitamin D. When almonds are consumed along with yogurt, the fats present in the nuts aid in the absorption of vitamin D efficiently. As per various studies, levels of vitamin D in the blood increases by 32 per cent when it is consumed with fats as compared to non-fats.

11. ***Chicken and carrots:*** Carrots have a lot of beta-carotene content that converts into vitamin A, which boosts immunity and is essential for the health of eyes and skin. On the other hand, chicken contains mineral zinc. But zinc has the ability to transform

beta-carotene into vitamin A; hence, the combination of carrots and chicken does wonder.

12. ***Cabbage family and fish:*** The cabbage family comprises of vegetables like broccoli, cauliflower, cabbage, and Brussels sprout, kale, etc. They contain plenty of sulforaphane compound—which has the ability to slow down the production of cancerous cells in the body. Whereas fish contains selenium. When the sulforaphane-enriched vegetables are eaten with selenium, the effect of sulforaphane increases tenfold.
13. ***Green tea and lemon:*** Green tea contains a high amount of catechin, a powerful antioxidant that fights high cholesterol, cancer, and cardiovascular diseases. When catechin is combined with some lemon, the acid in it helps absorb the antioxidants five times more than usual.
14. ***Turmeric and black pepper:*** Curcumin is the chief ingredient in turmeric, which acts as a powerful anti-inflammatory substance. It is quite helpful in preventing Alzheimer's disease, arthritis, cardiovascular diseases, etc. Piperine in black pepper increases the absorption of curcumin up to 2000 per cent. Usually, turmeric is not absorbed by the body, so its benefit cannot be reaped by an individual. But adding piperine in turmeric increases its bioavailability—the amount of a substance that's absorbed or can be used by the body—tremendously.

Combining Nutrients

1. ***Iron and vitamin C:*** Iron is better absorbed in the presence of vitamin C. Normally, the iron from animal-based foods is easily absorbed as compared to

iron from plant-based foods. Vitamin C breaks down the iron from the plants, making it easy for the body to absorb. Moreover, vitamin C helps in synthesising RBC (red blood cells), and iron is found in RBCs. This explains the relation between the two nutrients.

2. ***Quercetin and catechin:*** Quercetin is an anti-inflammatory pigment that is found in apples, onions, raspberries, etc., whereas catechin is an antioxidant that is found in grapes, green tea, and dark chocolate. When both quercetin and catechin are combined, they work to reduce the platelet aggression and atherosclerosis—a disease of arteries wherein fatty material deposits on the inner walls and leads to blockage.
3. ***Vitamin D and calcium:*** Calcium is properly utilised by the body only when the body has sufficient quantities of vitamin D. Vitamin D facilitates the absorption of calcium to develop healthy bones and teeth. In the case of vitamin D deficiency, calcium is wasted and not absorbed by the body. Hence, both nutrients go hand in hand.
4. ***Carotenoids and fats:*** Carotenoids are found in carrots, spinach, kale, sweet potatoes, etc. The fat present in them facilitates the easy absorption of carotenoids; hence, it must be had with fat-rich ingredients like nuts, grated cheese, or fat dressings on salads. This combination doesn't let carotenoids go to waste.
5. ***Apigenin and sulforaphane:*** Sulforaphane is a sulphur-based phytonutrient found in veggies like cabbage, Brussels sprout, cauliflower, broccoli, etc., and apigenin is a polyphenol that is found in apples, onions, leeks, grapes, tomatoes, tea, cherries, beans, etc. Both sulforaphane and apigenin, when taken separately, do

not help much. But when they are consumed together, their beneficial effect increases twelve times. All the above-mentioned vegetables can be combined in salads or stir-fried to gain maximum benefits.

6. ***Sulforaphane and selenium:*** The sources of sulforaphane are mentioned in Point 5, whereas selenium can be found in fish, poultry, and mushrooms. When both the nutrients are consumed together, their benefits and antioxidant power are multiplied tremendously.
7. ***Oils and fat-soluble vitamins (A, D, E, and K):*** Vitamins like A, D, E, and K are effectively absorbed by the body only in the presence of fats or oils. So, all the ingredients that are enriched in fat-soluble vitamins must be consumed with healthy fat sources like olive oil, walnut oil, etc.
   - **Vitamin A:** It helps in maintaining a healthy vision and is found in carrots, tomatoes, coloured peppers, and sweet potatoes.
   - **Vitamin D:** It helps in bone development and is found in eggs, dairy products, mushrooms, soya protein, and one of the most famous sources—sunlight.
   - **Vitamin E:** It acts as an antioxidant and is found in spinach, nuts, broccoli, vegetable oils like sunflower, safflower, and corn.
   - **Vitamin K:** It plays an important role in coagulation during injuries and is found in green leafy vegetables, Brussels sprout, etc.

Contradictory Foods—Foods at War

Irrespective of foods from the same or different groups, there are certain food combinations that should be strictly avoided. Foods that don't go together are considered to be foods at war. Certain food combinations actually hamper the functioning of the digestive system or don't allow other foods to be absorbed effectively. Such combinations are detrimental to one's health and must be avoided. If they are consumed together, they may lead to harmful effects and slow down your journey to better health. It means a few nutrients don't go with certain other nutrients; hence, they must not be consumed simultaneously. Thus, the concept of contradictory foods is equally important as compatible foods.

The guidelines mentioned below will help you understand the essence of foods at war easily:

1. ***Melon and any other food:*** Melons are a large family comprising several kinds of melons like watermelon, muskmelon, cantaloupe, and honeydew melon. Melon is quite easy to digest; as soon as it is consumed, it doesn't take long for it to digest. But when it is had with other fruits or food components, its digestion is delayed and gives a sense of uneasiness.

2. ***Milk and any other food:*** Milk is digested in the duodenum and not in the stomach. Milk consists of cream, which prohibits the gastric enzymes from releasing. Thus, when it is consumed with any other food, its digestion is delayed, causing discomfort.

   Milk with fish and meat is a complete no-no combination as both are ways apart in their temperament because milk is cold in nature while fish and meat are hot. Consuming both together creates hurdles for our body's channels and pollutes the blood as well. Consuming it with salt is also not desirable. Banana, too, doesn't go in harmony with milk as it leads to various allergies and cold & cough issues. Milk and bananas interfere with intestinal flora and may lead to mucous production which can cause cold, cough, and sinus congestion. Milk and watermelon, too, shouldn't be consumed together because milk takes longer to digest while melon is easy to digest and disrupts the digestion of milk. Milk should not be taken with citrus fruits as vitamin C in these fruits curdles milk and leads to various allergies.

3. ***Tomato and cucumber:*** Tomato is rich in vitamin C whereas cucumber has high water content and is easily digested. But cucumber has certain enzymes that don't allow the vitamin C in tomato to digest properly. Hence, this no-no combination results in flatulence, stomach ache, fatigue, and digestive uneasiness.
4. ***Tomato and cheese pasta:*** Tomato contains citric acid, which acts as a barrier to the digestion of starch in the pasta and protein in the cheese. Tomato even curdles the cheese—as it's a dairy product—in the stomach. In order to digest carb and protein simultaneously, it requires lot of energy and leads to discomfort. Hence, this combination should be avoided as much as possible.
5. ***Cucumber and lemon:*** Cucumber is cool in nature whereas lemon is hot. When eaten together, both try to act according to their potency, i.e. cucumber tries to cool lemon and lemon attempts to heat cucumber. Hence, they produce toxic compounds that are not desirable for a proper digestive system. Hence, they should be avoided, too.

Nutrients and Foods to Avoid Consuming Together

1. ***Avoid eating acidic and carbohydrate foods together***

   Examples of carbs are potatoes, peas, bananas,

beans, breads, etc., whereas the acidic foods comprise citric fruits like lemon, lime, orange, kiwifruit, pineapple, tomato, amla, tamarind, or any other sour fruits. The digestion of any food is based on its acidic or alkaline nature. Carbohydrate is digested by ptyalin, an enzyme present in the saliva, and it acts best in alkaline medium. In fact, ptyalin breaks down the starch into simple sugars and is further broken down in the small intestine for proper digestion. When an acidic food is consumed with carbohydrate, the acetic acid—found in vinegar, citric acid—found in citrus fruits, malic acid—found in apples, peaches, plums, etc., tartaric acid—found in grapes, oxalic acid—found in berries—doesn't allow the carbohydrate to be digested. Such acid hampers the breakdown of carbohydrate and leads to its fermentation.

When there is hyperacidity in the stomach, the carbohydrate is not digested easily. Thus, the combination of acidic and carbohydrate foods is an example of incompatible foods.

2. ***Avoid protein and carbohydrate foods together***

Protein and carbohydrate are two macronutrients, and they hamper each other's digestion if consumed together as they are of different temperaments. The gastric juices, a combination of pepsin and hydrochloric acid, aid in digesting protein—by an acidic process—and saliva aids in digesting carbohydrate—by an alkaline process. Both these processes are never in harmony. The consumption of protein releases gastric juices that raises the acidity level in the stomach and delays the carb digestion, thus, the carb starts fermenting, which is undesirable. Carb consumption restricts the release of gastric juices as well, hampering with the digestion of protein. The undigested starch absorbs enzyme pepsin and destroys ptyalin, which increases hydrochloric acids in the stomach, thereby increasing acidity.

So, protein- and carbohydrate-based foods should not be consumed together.

3. *Avoid two heavy protein-based foods together*

Protein is present in almost everything we eat, but the food that is loaded with protein should not be consumed with other protein-based products. For example, avoid meat with eggs or nuts, eggs with cheese and milk, or cheese with nuts and eggs. All protein-based foods have distinct nature, composition, and character. Moreover, all these foods are digested by different digestive juices—pancreatic juices. It is advised to consume only one protein-based food in a meal like have either meat or cheese or eggs or nuts.

4. *Avoid concentrated proteins and fats together*

Consumption of fat slows down the release of gastric juices that are required for protein foods like meat, nuts, eggs, etc. Fat in the stomach delays the production of pancreatic juices. In simple words, fats are responsible for decreasing the function of gastric glands and juices—pepsin and hydrochloric acid—thereby hampering the digestion process of protein.

5. *Avoid protein with acidic fruits*

The acidic content in fruits restricts the release of gastric juices, which are required for smooth protein digestion. So, it is advisable to avoid eating acidic fruits like pineapples, lemons, oranges along with meat or eggs.

6. ***Avoid starch and sugar together***

Many foods are available in the market that are either coated in starch or sugar or both. But various starch-based products like cereal, potato, and bread should be avoided with jellies, jams, honey, molasses, or sugar. Whenever sugar is consumed, it has a tendency to stop the release of ptyalin, which is essential for the digestion of starch- or carb-based foods. In such cases, the fermentation of starch begins, leading to uneasiness in the stomach.

Note: *It is very evident from certain instances that the digestive juices or enzymes required for the digestion of carbohydrate or protein should not be hampered in any way. In case they are not given a favourable environment, the balance of acid-alkaline will be at risk. The proper balance of acidity and alkalinity in stomach defines the growth of several healthy cells, keeping various diseases at bay.*

Each nutrient has its own rule of digestion. If any other element enters in the territory of other food component during the period of digestion, it acts differently. Based entirely on the immune and digestive system, they are absorbed and digested by the body. An individual with efficient digestive power can digest almost anything without any discomfort, but as one ages, this power may weaken gradually. But if the right principles are followed in life, the functioning of digestive system can be great for a long time, resulting in splendid health benefits. More heed needs to be paid on the characteristics of compatible and incompatible foods for a healthy body and blissful living.

10
Vegetarianism vs Non-Vegetarianism

'Nothing will benefit health and increase the chances for survival of earth as the evolution to a vegetarian diet.'

—Albert Einstein

The food available all across the globe can be broadly categorised into two varieties: Vegetarian and non-vegetarian. It is a matter of gargantuan debate whether one variety is healthier than the other. Distinct schools of thought appear and they justify their diet; hence, it is left to an individual to opt for either a vegetarian or non-vegetarian diet as per their wish and what suits them.

The aspect of being vegetarian and non-vegetarian is not just a matter of choice, but many factors have played a huge role in deciding one's diet plan. We will not be delving deep into this specific perspective, rather we will be focussing on the pros and cons of both the diet preferences.

Vegetarianism

Vegetarian diet is further divided into divisions like pure vegetarian, lacto-vegetarian and lacto-ovo-vegetarian, ovo-vegetarian, herbivores, fruitarians, raw/living foodists, pesco-vegetarian, pollo-vegetarian, and demi-vegetarians. Pure vegetarians eat all types of vegetables, fruits, nuts, legumes, and grains. Lacto-vegetarians eat all plant-based foods and dairy products. Lacto-ovo-vegetarians consume animal products such as eggs and cheese along with plants and dairy products.

Below are vegetarian sub-categories:

- Pure vegetarian diet—All Vegetables + Fruits + Legumes + Nuts + Grains
- Lacto-vegetarian diet—All Plant foods + Dairy Products
- Lacto-ovo vegetarian diet—Lacto-vegetarian diet + Eggs
- Ovo-vegetarian diet—All foods + Eggs (no meat, fish, seafood, or dairy products)
- Pescatarian—All foods + Dairy Products + Eggs + Fish (no meat)
- Herbivores—Only plant foods
- Fruitarians—Only fruits
- Raw/living foodists—About 75 per cent uncooked, unprocessed, organic fruits and vegetables

Apart from this, veganism is another way of living that excludes all animal products and their by-products. Vegans abstain from eating meat, fish, poultry, eggs, dairy products, honey, fats obtained from animals, gelatinc, and any animal protein, etc.

Benefits of a Vegetarian Diet

1. A vegetarian diet is low-fat food and minimises the chances of coronary and cardiovascular diseases

2. It reduces the chances of obesity as it helps maintain or reduce weight due to its low-fat content
3. It protects from several cancers
4. It helps in controlling blood sugar, thereby preventing diabetes
5. It lowers the possibility of blood pressure issues and boosts blood flow
6. It controls cholesterol levels
7. It reduces oxidative stress and inflammation in the body
8. It also minimises the chance of chronic kidney diseases
9. It reduces the probabilities of food poisoning
10. Foods like green leafy vegetables, wheat bran, and cheese are loaded with vitamin K, which helps in coagulation
11. Dairy products and green leafy vegetables are full of calcium and result in better health of teeth and bones
12. Cereals, pulses, fruits, and salt are rich in minerals like sodium and potassium, which are required for proper functioning of nerves and muscles. These foods also help in maintain proper water balance in the body

Disadvantages of a Vegetarian Diet

1. A vegetarian diet is not so protein-efficient in nature. In fact, certain complete proteins are not available in such a diet. Complete proteins are formed when nine essential amino acids are present in the food, but plant-based foods hardly contain all essential amino acids

2. It has also been observed that the elderly may encounter calorie deficiency due to adhering to a vegetarian diet. It does contain certain nutrients but in lower quantities
3. Vitamin B12 is present in animal-based foods; so, a deficiency of this vitamin may also occur due to a strictly vegetarian diet
4. Vegetarians are advised to keep a check on the consumption of nutrients like zinc, vitamin D, iodine, iron, and Omega-3 fatty acids as they are not available much in a plant-based diet
5. Creatine—an amino acid made by other amino acids like arginine, methionine, glycine—is used by muscles and is found in meat and fish. Hence, a strictly vegetarian diet may also lead to its deficiency. Creatine supplements are easily available in the market

Non-Vegetarianism

A non-vegetarian diet includes chicken, meat, fish, eggs along with plant-based foods and animal by-products. A Non-vegetarian diet is broad and lavish in its list of food ingredients as compared to a vegetarian diet. It includes the meat of chicken, turkey, quail, partridge, deer, lamb, sheep, beef, veal, and pig along with various varieties of fish and shellfish. It also includes animal by-products like milk, eggs, animal fats, rennet, and gelatine. Thus, anyone who consumes meat is known as non-vegetarian.

Below are non-vegetarian sub-categories:

- Pescatarian or pesco-vegetarian—All foods + Dairy Products + Eggs + Fish (no other meats)
- Pollo-vegetarian—poultry (no beef)
- Demi-vegetarian—Fish with little or no meat

Benefits of a Non-Vegetarian Diet

1. Non-vegetarian diets are a good source of proteins and phosphorus
2. It supports body tissues in rebuilding and repairing. It also maximises the production of antibodies and red blood cells in the body, thereby protecting us from various infections
3. It promotes and maintains strong teeth and is highly beneficial for skin, eyes, and brain development
4. As it is a rich source of various vitamins, it helps in normal functioning of the body system
5. Being a rich source of protein and fats, it is essential in building strong bones and muscles
6. As selenium and zinc are found in abundance in animal products, it increases metabolism and facilitates breakdown of fats
7. Seafood is a great source of nutrients responsible for promoting brain health
8. Vitamin B12 and iron are ample in non-vegetarian products, especially eggs, milk, meat, and fish. This vitamin is essential for the formation of red blood cells and proper functioning of the nerves. In case one has a deficiency of both the said nutrients, she/he may experience severe fatigue, loss of body balance, and even shortness of breath

Disadvantages of a Non-Vegetarian Diet

1. A non-vegetarian diet may increase the likelihood of high blood pressure, cholesterol issues, and cardiovascular diseases.

2. It may lead to constipation, hypertension, and obesity
3. Various studies claim that animals for slaughter usually survive in conditions of fear; hence, consuming their meat may lead to anger, fear, and stress
4. Many a time, animals are injected with drugs and hormones in order to favour their growth. Such medications may be transmitted to people following a non-vegetarian diet, increasing the risk of mental disorders.
5. A non-vegetarian diet may also result to lower stamina in the body
6. It has been studied that after consuming a non-vegetarian meal, high alkaline salts are excreted through urine from the body, and this can lead to the weakening of bones
7. It is believed that one sticking to this diet preference may have a shorter lifespan with more probability of chronic diseases

Thus, both vegetarian and non-vegetarian diets have their pros and cons, and it is just up to us to decide what we must consume for overall health and fitness. In both the cases, we need to be more alert to overcome the demerits of each diet to ensure our well-being. The excess of anything is detrimental to our health, and the best way to move towards a healthy lifestyle is *balance*.

11

Microgreens

'If you are growing microgreens you need to use a blue spectrum light instead of red. When growing any kind of plants, blue light is used for growth while red is used for flowering.'

—Nick Jones

Microgreens are, undoubtedly, the latest blessings to the humankind from the world of nutrients. These are young vegetable greens that have an aromatic flavour. They are harvested a little less than two to three weeks—depending upon the variety—after sprouting. Microgreens attain a height of about 1–2 inches and are available in an array of colours and textures.

These edible tiny plants are dense in flavour and nutritive value. They are bound to surprise your plate with a burst of zest, colour, and texture. These tiny plants range between sprouts and baby greens. The only difference between sprouts and microgreens is that sprouts do not have leaves. The right time to harvest microgreens is when the first leaves are spotted.

They can be grown from a wide variety of plants like cauliflower, broccoli, cabbage, radish, lettuce, chicory, dill, carrot, celery, garlic, onion, beet, fenugreek, spinach, cucumber, melon, etc.; cereals like rice, oats, barley, and wheat, etc.; and legumes like beans, peas, lentils, etc.

When it comes to microgreens, only the leaves and stems are edible, whereas roots and seeds are not consumed. They are grown in slightly less warm and humid conditions, and the best part is that they can be easily grown at home.

Incorporating microgreens is easy in dishes like sandwiches, salads, pizzas, soups, omelettes, curries, and even in smoothies and juices. Microgreens can find their way in any dish. They add a whole new dimension to the aspect of flavour of the food; moreover, they can also be used as a garnish.

Some facts and trends of microgreens:

- Wheatgrass juice is one of the latest juice trends in many parts of the country
- Broccoli microgreens are believed to contain 500 per cent of the daily requirement of nutrients like minerals—magnesium, iron, and phosphorus—and vitamins—A, B, C, E, and K.
- The microgreens of wheatgrass, basil, radish, sunflower shoots, pea shoots, etc., also have proved their worth in terms of high density of nutrients
- Lettuce and chicory are high in vitamin A or carotenoid antioxidants
- The microgreens of red cabbage contain around 40 times more vitamin E and 6 times more vitamin C as compared to mature and fully grown red cabbage
- The microgreens of green coriander contain around three times more lutein (phytochemicals) and beta-carotene as compared to mature green coriander

The most popular varieties of microgreens are produced from:

- **Brassicaceae family:** Cauliflower, broccoli, cabbage, watercress, radish and arugula
- **Asteraceae family:** Lettuce, endive, chicory and radicchio
- **Apiaceae family:** Dill, carrot, fennel and celery
- **Amaryllidaceae family:** Garlic, onion, leek
- **Amaranthaceae family**: Amaranth, quinoa, swiss chard, beet and spinach
- **Cucurbitaceae family:** Melon, cucumber and squash

Benefits of Microgreens

1. Microgreens are compact form of foods that are overloaded with high-density nutrients. They consist of a wide variety of nutrients—around 4 to 40 times more—like minerals and vitamins as compared to fully grown plants. They are so packed with micronutrients that only their small serving is required to provide the daily requirement of vitamins and minerals. Swiss chard contains a high content of vitamin K, A, and C, whereas beetroots have high content of manganese and folate.

2. Microgreens are overloaded with polyphenols—a natural chemical present in various foods and are recognised for the quality of antioxidants. Polyphenols are also known to reduce the chances of heart diseases, Alzheimer's, and even cancer. Microgreens consist of a variety of polyphenols as compared to its fully grown mature plants. Other sources of polyphenols are: Fruits, vegetables, chocolate, tea, and coffee.

3. Microgreens are also capable of reducing weight, LDL cholesterol, and triglyceride levels; hence, they are blessed with the quality to improve heart health. An individual on a microgreen-rich diet is less prone to heart issues. Incorporating microgreens along with a regular workout regime can keep one hale and hearty.
4. Microgreens have been accepted medically as well. Consuming vegetables reduce the possibility of certain cancers, especially prostate cancer and cancer related to the digestive tract. They also relieve one from inflammation and the possibility of diseases like diabetes; fenugreek is especially known for this.
5. In India, it has been found that around 70–80 per cent of the population suffers from the deficiency of some or the minerals and vitamins. The consumption of microgreens helps in overcoming this deficiency.

Microgreens have been and can be a great addition to the concept of high-density nutrients. They are considered to be great antioxidants that can help fight free radicals. They may be tiny but are full of nutrients as mentioned above. Easy to grow and easy to handle, they are no less than a blessing for humanity as they keep several diseases at bay. Microgreens are great superfoods and it is best to incorporate them in your diet.

Part II

SUPERFOODS

12
Onions

'I will not move my army without onions!'
—Ulysses S. Grant

Onion is one of the most common ingredients used in almost every kitchen. It is a member of the allium family and is associated with scallions, garlic, chives, leeks, and shallots. It is available in different sizes and varieties and is packed with several medicinal properties and therapeutic values. Onions in the bulbing stage are called scallions or spring onions or green onions.

Onion comprises of various phytonutrients, sulphur compounds, and phenolic compounds. It has biotin, vitamin B6, quercetin, vitamin C, dietary fibre, and many other minerals. It won't be wrong to state that this superfood provides numerous benefits. It can be consumed in any form—raw or cooked form; sliced or pureed. Its benefits can also be derived in the form of fresh juices.

Onion has antibiotic, antipyretic—that inhibits or reduces fever, anti-microbial—that destroys the disease-carrying microorganisms, anti-asthmatic, and anti-inflammatory properties. Consumption of onion on a daily basis also helps in osteoporosis—a condition in which bones become brittle due to loss of tissue—and atherosclerosis—a disease of arteries wherein deposition of fatty material takes place in inner walls. It is even used for eye and ear disorders. It is also helpful in rejuvenating body tissues. Moreover, it is also used in various beauty treatments. Thus, onion has many therapeutic qualities and is, undoubtedly, a boon to humankind.

Some of the features of onions are:

- Onion has plenty of quercetin, a plant pigment that comprises of powerful antioxidants. It has a unique power to fight and prevent cancer, especially stomach or colon cancer.
- When one is stressed, cortisol is released. And when it is in excess, it leads to muscle tissue damage and is responsible for protein breakdown in the body as well. Quercetin has the ability to suppress enzymes that are required for the release of cortisol, thereby providing relief during stress.

  Other sources of quercetin are: Apples, amla, berries, red wine, green tea, broccoli, pepper, grapes, etc.
- Onion also has the ability to lower the cholesterol levels by increasing the good cholesterol, i.e. HDL (High Density Lipoprotein).

  Raw onion does this job, so it is desirable to consume raw onion in salads, etc.
- It is loaded with vitamin C, which helps boost the immune system.
- Onions contain betalains, a plant pigment that helps in joint pain and arthritis. It has anti-inflammatory properties. It also helps in reducing the swelling in joints.

Other sources of betalains are: Beetroot, rhubarb, chard, red amaranth, red pears, red pitahaya.

- It has sufficient quantities of biotin (Vitamin B7). Biotin, when combined with mineral chromium, can help regulate blood sugar and reduce resistance to insulin; thus, helping in controlling diabetes. Biotin improves skin and hair quality and texture; it also strengthens nails.

  Other sources of chromium are: Potatoes, whole grains, broccoli, meat, seafood, liver, egg yolk, and mushrooms.

- Onion also has the quality to strengthen the bone density in older, especially menopausal, women.
- Onion contains sulphur, which helps in thinning the blood that helps in preventing heart attack or stroke. The clogging of blood increases the possibility of such cardiovascular attacks. Thus, onion lowers one's blood pressure and safeguards the heart.
- Onion contains a lot of fibre, which is important for a healthy digestive system as it releases digestive juices. So, consume as much onion as possible in its raw form.
- It is loaded with vitamin A and C, which act as anti-ageing elements.
- Onion is packed with soluble fibres called fructans, which also act as prebiotic fibres, feeding gut bacteria.

  Other sources of fructans are: Fruits like dates, ripe bananas, plums, raisins, and pomegranate; vegetables like leeks, shallots, snow peas, beets, artichoke, and asparagus.

- Onion is also believed to relieve insomnia. It is said that including one whole onion in a meal provides relief in insomnia conditions.

- It also has carminative properties; hence, it relives flatulence.
- Onion seeds, also known as Nigella seeds, are also blessed with great medicinal properties. They have thymoquinone—phytochemical compound that acts as an antioxidant that has analgesic (pain relieving material or drug) and anticonvulsant (that prevents or reduces epileptic fits) properties.
- Onion seeds also have anti-cancerous and anti-asthmatic properties.

Note: *Avoid over-peeling onions as the most crucial flavonoids are lost due to this. Over-peeling results in a 20 per cent loss of quercetin and about 70 per cent loss of anthocyanins. Onion has been a rich source of polyphenols—phytonutrients group containing flavonoids and tannins—and is extremely good for health. In order to derive its maximum benefits, it needs to be cooked on low-heat and for a longer period. It is advised to sauté thick onion slices for a short time. An individual must consume around 150 gm of onion on a daily basis.*

Trivia

Onion contains volatile oil chemically known as allyl propyl disulfide ($C_3H_5S_2C_3H_7$). This particular oil constituent is responsible for the pungency of onions, which can vary from mild to extremely pungent.

Have you ever wondered why your eyes tear up while cutting onion? It is because of a chemical irritant, propanethial-S-oxide is released, which irritates the eyes.

Nutritive Highlights

Onion is known for its low-calorie content as it contains only 40 calories in 100 gm. As far as nutrients are concerned, onion consists of:

- 89 per cent water
- 1.1 per cent protein
- 9.3 per cent carbohydrate
- 4.2 per cent sugar
- 1.7 per cent fibre
- 0.1 per cent negligible low-fat

13
Flaxseeds

'Wherever flaxseeds become a regular food item among the people, there will be better health.'
—Mahatma Gandhi

Flaxseeds, also known as linseeds, are the seeds of the flax plant. They are mostly golden or tan brown in colour. Flaxseed oil is obtained from flaxseeds and is a rich source of healthy fats that are easy to digest. It has been researched that flaxseeds, when grounded coarsely, can be stored for about ten months at room temperature. The most important thing is that during storage no loss of Omega-3 fatty acids is observed. These wonder seeds, when baked at a temperature of about 150°C for 3 hours, don't have any effect on the Omega-3 fatty acid content. Flaxseeds have numerous benefits and are highly regarded for their high-fibre content and low carbohydrates.

Some of the features of flaxseeds are:

- Flaxseeds are exceptional in their content of high mucilage—a thick and sticky consistency secretion—gum content, and is easily water-soluble. Due to this property, they move undigested through the gastrointestinal tract. When consumed, they remain in the stomach, retaining the food with it, and do not allow the food to shift to the small intestine, thereby allowing maximum nutrient absorption along with providing a feeling of satiety.

- Low in carbohydrate content, they are a great source of soluble and insoluble fibre. Fibre-enriched flaxseeds perform the role of colon detoxification in an exceptional manner. It also promotes fat loss and even reduces sugar cravings.
- Omega-3 fatty acid is one of the best nutrients found in flaxseeds. It is clinically proven that alpha-lipoic acid, which is present in Omega-3 fatty acid, aids in decreasing the risk of coronary diseases and relieves one from hypertension as well. Apart from this, it is also responsible for improving the functionality of platelets and is anti-inflammatory in nature.

  Omega-3 fatty acids and its sources: Omega-3 fatty acids are of three types, and they are found in both plant and animal food sources. They are available in walnuts, kidney beans, soyabean oil, chia seeds, hemp seeds, algae, and seaweed; and in fish and fish oils. Omega-3 surrounds every cell in our body, making it an important component of the body. It performs many functions such as improving the immune system and providing energy to the body, along with improving several other functions in heart, lungs, and blood vessels.
- Omega-3 fatty acid is a great nutrient as it provides one with essential fatty acids and some vitamin B, which are required for the better health of skin and hair. It decreases the dryness and flakiness of the skin and provides a huge relief in acne and eczema. It is also helpful in dry eye syndrome, as it acts as a great lubricant.

- It has been proven that consuming flaxseeds can increase the amount of fat to be excreted through the bowel movements, thereby reducing cholesterol levels naturally. The fibre content present in flaxseeds is soluble in water that can trap the fat and cholesterol in the digestive system and, then, excrete it through the bowel movement. The soluble fibre also holds bile, made from cholesterol in the gall bladder. Bile is then removed from the digestive system, lowering the cholesterol level.
- Few people are sensitive to gluten, and this gluten intolerance is referred to as celiac disease. In this condition, people find it hard to digest gluten containing flour like wheat, etc. Flaxseeds have emerged as a substitute to gluten and it can be easily digested by those suffering from celiac disease.

  Other sources of gluten are: Rye, barley, malted milk, malt vinegar, brewer's yeast, and wheatgrass.
- Flaxseeds are loaded with a lot of lignans—a fibre related to polyphenols—and act as antioxidants and fight free radicals effectively. They also help in anti-ageing, balancing hormones, and repairing cells damaged by free radicals.
- Lignans have the power of natural phytoestrogens or plant nutrients, acting similar to oestrogen. The phytoestrogens available in flaxseeds are able to change the oestrogen metabolism or hormonal status of an individual.
- Lignans have amazing antiviral and antibacterial properties. Due to this, they are quite effective in treating common cold.

- Lignans also boost the growth of probiotics in the stomach. They are also effective in removing yeast and candida—a yeast-like fungus responsible for mouth and throat infections.

  Other sources of lignans are: Pumpkin seeds, sunflower seeds, poppy seeds, sesame seeds, wheat, oats, rye, and berries.

- Flaxseeds are beneficial in promoting digestive health. The Omega-3 fatty acids reduce inflammation and act as protective layer for the gastrointestinal tract. They are also enormously beneficial if one has Crohn's disease (Chronic inflammatory disease existing in intestines).

- At times, the level of fats and lipids in the blood increases tremendously, which is called hyperlipidaemia. This increases the chances of ischemic heart disease—— insufficient supply of blood to an organ especially heart muscles. Flaxseeds play a prominent role in lowering these harmful lipids.

- Various studies have affirmed that flaxseeds are capable of reducing the possibility of cancer. The lignans present in them can be converted into oestrogen by intestinal bacteria, thereby balancing the hormones in the body naturally. Balanced hormones majorly decrease the chances of breast and ovarian cancer along with several other issues in women. It also reduces the possibility of osteoporosis in women.

Note: *Flaxseeds are more effective in providing benefits when they are consumed in grounded form. Soaking them in water for, at least, 10 minutes and then grinding them is recommended. If consumed whole, the body cannot derive all the nutrients present in them, as whole seeds mostly go undigested in the intestinal* *tract. It is said that, in an adult, about 25–40 gm of fibre should come from foods that are high in fibre content, whereas consuming just 2 tablespoons of flaxseeds provide around 20 per cent of the fibre requirements. It is recommended to include flaxseeds in breakfast along with sufficient water. It can also be sprouted and then consumed. Eating sprouted flaxseeds helps in better mineral absorption.*

Flaxseeds have blood-thinning properties, so they should be avoided prior to a surgery. They should also be avoided when a person is on diabetes medication as it lowers the blood sugar quite a bit. It also lowers the blood pressure, so this must also be kept in mind.

Nutritive Highlights

Flaxseeds are rich in calories and contain around 534 calories in 100 gm. They are rich in calcium, iron, vitamin B6, and magnesium as well. They are also packed with:

- 42 per cent fat (29 per cent polyunsaturated fats, 8 per cent monounsaturated fats, and 3.7 per cent saturated fats)
- 0 cholesterol
- 29 per cent carbohydrate (27 per cent dietary fibre and 1.6 per cent sugar)
- 18 per cent protein

14
Beetroot

'The beet is the most intense of vegetables.'
—Tom Robbins

Beetroots, also known as beets, are root vegetables that are available in many varieties and are identified by their colours such as white, yellow, pink, or dark purple. The most common are the reddish-purple beetroots. Gifted with numerous benefits, beetroots can be consumed raw, cooked, or as a juice; in fact, they can even be pickled. Even the leaves of beets are known as beet greens, which are edible. They are a concentrated source of vitamins, minerals, and carotenoids, hence, consumed by many.

Certain beets are rich in sugar-content and are used for extracting beet sugar, but they are different from the beetroots we are going to talk about.

Some of the features of beets are:

- Beetroots are a rich source of betalains. Betalains in beetroots are of two types—betanin and vulgaxanthin and both are great antioxidants. Betalains have great anti-inflammatory qualities and are also useful in the detoxification of the body. Betalains are lost when they are exposed to long cooking period, so, in order to avail optimum benefits of this plant pigment, it should be steamed for not more than 15 minutes and roasted for not more than an hour.

Other sources of betalains are: Onion, red amaranth, red pears, chard, rhubarb, and red pitahaya.

- Betanin pigments available in beetroots restrict the production of pro-inflammatory enzymes. It has been studied that this is responsible for reducing the growth of tumour cells in the colon, stomach, lung, breast, prostate, and nerves.

  Note: *Not all individuals can absorb and digest betalains from beets. Those who can derive the benefits are known as 'betalain responders', and such people are around 20 per cent across the globe. After the consumption of beetroot, the reddening of urine occurs and this reddening of urine is termed as beeturia. It is not a harmful occurrence, but it indicates the slight possibility of iron deficiency or excessive iron or even an issue towards iron metabolism in the body.*

- The undesired and long inflammation also results in several diseases like heart diseases and even atherosclerosis—build-up of fatty material on inner walls of arteries. Constant inflammation is also the reason for diabetes. The anti-inflammatory properties of beetroots are of great help to control these chronic diseases.

  The nitric oxide in beetroots improves the blood flow by dilating the blood vessels, making it good for the blood flow. It reduces arterial diseases like atherosclerosis.

- Betaine is a pivotal nutrient present in beetroots. It is made from choline—a basic compound present in living tissues. Choline is able to regulate inflammation in the body and stops the production of compound homocysteine (amino acid), which is responsible for harmful chronic inflammation and heart diseases, too. So, consuming beetroots helps in anti-inflammatory conditions.

Other sources of betaine are: Spinach, wheat, and shellfish.

- Choline, which is present in beetroots, helps in sleep conditions, better muscle movement, and promotes better memory and learning. It maintains the structure of cellular membranes and also helps in fat absorption of the body. It is also effective in fighting chronic inflammation.

  Other sources of choline are: Eggs, peanut, spinach, meat, fish, poultry, and wheat.

- It is believed that the alpha-lipoic acid, an antioxidant present in beetroot, lowers the glucose levels and increases the insulin sensibility along with preventing oxidative stress-induced changes in a diabetic person.
- With age, the blood flow to several parts of the brain decreases and this results in reduced mental action, which can lead to diseases like dementia. Beetroot juice has ample nitrate, which can improve the blood flow along with oxygenating the areas with less blood flow, thereby delaying dementia.
- As nitrate in beetroot is known to be effective in blood flow and oxygenation of muscles, it is beneficial in increasing endurance. It actually improves the quality of cardiovascular and respiratory activities by oxygenating the affected areas of the body.
- As beetroot is high in fibre content, it reduces the chances of constipation, leading to better gut health.

- As beets are packed with potassium, it helps in reducing hair loss. Moreover, it protects hair as well as keeps the skin hydrated for long. It acts as an anti-ageing ingredient.
- It also removes toxins from the body by promoting detoxification, thus, making it healthy for the liver. It contains glutathione (antioxidant), which avoids damage to the liver. It also promotes regeneration of liver cells and also improves the formation of fats within the liver.
- Beets help prevent anaemia as it increases the level of haemoglobin in the blood, as it is a rich source of iron.
- Beetroot juice is alkaline in nature and helps in reducing the condition of acidosis in the stomach. Hence, it improves the digestive system.

Nutritive Highlights

Beetroots have low calorific value and consist of even less than 45 calories in 100 gm. They are loaded with micronutrients like folate, vitamin B6, vitamin A and C, pantothenic acid, potassium, manganese, copper, iron, sodium, betaine, and choline. It is also rich in fibre. They consist of:

- 87 per cent water
- 9.6 per cent carbohydrate
- 6.8 per cent sugar
- 2.8 per cent fibre
- 1.6 per cent protein
- 0.2 per cent fat

15
Garlic

'Garlic is divine. Few food items can taste so many distinct ways, handled correctly. Misuse of garlic is a crime . . . Please, treat your garlic with respect.'

—Anthony Bourdain

Garlic, a member of the allium family, is associated with onion, scallions, chives, leeks, and shallots. All of these are known for their pungency and excellent flavour. Garlic is a culinary spice whose medicinal values have been known for aeons. Humankind has been fortunate to have this priceless ingredient to serve them in innumerable ailments and disorders. It is also used for its prophylactic—which prevent diseases—characteristic, along with great culinary usage and healing approach.

The single segment of garlic is known as clove and the whole head is called garlic bulb. A bulb of garlic has around 10–20 cloves. The building block of DNA and RNA is present more in garlic as compared to any other food. Garlic is a rich source of around ten different types of natural sugars like fructose, glucose, inulin, etc. Garlic is rich in almost thirty-three sulphur compounds like alliin, allicin, allyl propyl disulfide, etc., seventeen different amino acids, and various minerals like selenium and other trace minerals.

Garlic's benefits are enormous and this ingredient is worth incorporating in one's diet. It is renowned for its anti-cancer and anti-tumour properties. It also keeps the heart in perfect health and prevents stroke, blood pressure, and atherosclerosis. It also acts as an antiviral, antibacterial, and antimicrobial. It has the power to control diabetes as well. It increases stamina and performance of an individual. It also acts as an outstanding aphrodisiac, thereby improving sexual desire and health. Thus, in order to be free from certain diseases and disorders, including garlic in one's diet is a must. The best part about garlic is that it can be easily incorporated in one's diet—it can be used in curries, tempering, dips, salads, or can be eaten raw.

Some of the features of garlic are:

- The organosulfur compound, allicin and diallyl disulfide—present in garlic oil—are available in large amounts in garlic. These compounds are beneficial in cardiovascular health of an individual. It has been proven clinically that consuming garlic is effective in lowering blood pressure, reducing blood cholesterol and triglyceride level, restricting platelet collection, and preventing atherosclerosis.
- It also increases the HDL (good cholesterol) and reduces the harmful LDL (bad cholesterol), blood cholesterol, and triglyceride. This effect towards balancing cholesterol acts as a protective mechanism towards cardiovascular health.
- Garlic has been found to prevent thrombosis—clotting of blood in part of circulatory system, thereby ensuring proper blood flow and better cardiovascular activities.

- Garlic is effective in metabolising iron as the diallyl disulfide present in it helps in increasing the production of protein called ferroportin. Actually, ferroportin runs throughout the cell membrane and creates a passage that permits stored iron in the body to leave the cells and get consumed where it is required.
- Garlic has sulphur molecules called polysulfides, which are consumed by red blood cells, and they produce hydrogen sulfide. Hydrogen sulfide facilitates our blood vessels to expand and contract, keeping a check on blood pressure.

  Note: *Garlic in processed foods is incapable of producing hydrogen sulfide, making it ineffective.*
- Garlic contains a sulphur compound called 1, 2-vinyldithiin, which can act as an anti-inflammatory. Garlic consumption regulates the number of fat cells that are synthesised in our body. The sulphur compound in garlic inhibits this fat conversion and controls inflammatory system activity. The low inflammation leads to obesity in certain individuals and garlic is beneficial in relieving ailments caused by it.
- Garlic prevents any blockage in our blood vessels along with avoiding clots from being formed inside the vessels. A volatile oil with sulphur compound called ajoene is associated with this aspect. Ajoene has strong anti-clotting features. It also helps in preventing certain cells from becoming too sticky in our blood and lowers the risk of platelets getting together to form a clot.
- Garlic has also been recognised for the extraordinary feature of being antibacterial and antiviral in nature, too. The disulfide compound present in garlic ajoene is beneficial in preventing the infections along with

yeast candida albicans. It is effective wherein the body has become resistant to the bacterial infections that are being treated with prescriptions of antibiotics for a longer duration.

- Generally, it is a small piece of protein (angiotensin II) that aids in contracting blood vessels. When this happens, blood is forced to pass through thinner vessels, hence, increasing the blood pressure. But the allicin present in garlic helps in blocking the activity of angiotensin II, reducing the possibility of an increase in blood pressure.
- Garlic contains a good amount of vitamin B6, which helps in reducing homocysteine levels. It is believed that homocysteine is responsible for damaging the walls of the blood vessels.
- Garlic is also known and revered for being anti-cancer in nature. It has been proven that high consumption of garlic is responsible for lowering the risk of all cancers, except for prostate and breast cancer. On the other hand, moderate consumption is responsible in lowering the colorectal and renal cancer. Hence, it can easily be classified as an anti-cancer food.
- Whenever meat is cooked at a temperature of more than 200°C, a harmful cancer-related substance called heterocyclic amines (HCAs) is released. These HCAs gets transformed into carcinogens and are responsible for the reason behind breast cancer. But garlic contains diallyl sulfide, which is known to inhibit the growth of HCAs, which in turn helps in reducing the chances of breast cancer.
- Garlic helps in improving the performance of an individual and reducing fatigue. For ages, it has been

consumed by those who are involved in heavy work and athletes.

- It also acts as an aphrodisiac, resulting in a better sexual desire and health.

Trivia

The sulphur compound present in garlic is 'allicin' and it is considered for imparting garlic its pungent aroma and taste. The therapeutic effects of garlic are believed to be because of this so-called allicin. Allinase, an enzyme, is activated whenever garlic is chopped or crushed, which results in the production of a compound known as allicin— from alliin— that is already present in garlic.

Nutritive Highlights

Garlic is bountiful in numerous compounds. This versatile ingredient provides 98 calories in 100 gm. It is also enriched with vitamin B6 (pyridoxine) and minerals like manganese, selenium, and vitamin C, along with iron, copper, calcium, potassium, and phosphorus. It consists of:

- 16.3 per cent carbohydrate
- 5.5 per cent fibre
- 0.6 per cent fat

16

Ginger

'Every time I feel like something is missing from a dish, I think, "Oh, I know, I'll add a pinch of dry ginger." If it's not salt and it's not vinegar, it's probably missing dry ginger.'

—Alex Guarnaschelli

Ginger is a rhizome, they grow perpendicular, permitting new shoots to grow up out of the ground, and a member of the Zingiberaceae family. It is most commonly used as a spice for its exceptional culinary worth and medicinal properties. Incorporating ginger in our diet is quite easy as it can be used in tea and curries as well. It is versatile in nature and it can be used to flavour both sweet and savoury items—in various marinades for meat and fish, in salad dressings, soups, smoothies, baked desserts, tea, and cocktails. Apart from using it fresh, it is also used in dried, pickled, preserved, crystallised, candied, and powdered forms. It can be chopped, sliced, grated, or even pureed, depending on the dish where it is being added.

Ginger also contains aromatic compounds like zingiberene and bisabolene. Moreover, it has a certain pungency, odour, and flavour due to the presence of volatile oils such as gingerols and shogaols.

Some of the features of ginger are:

- Ginger is a boon for the gut as the chemical compounds present in it provide relief in stomach ache and facilitates better digestion, too. It improves the digestion system if consumed in a small amount just before a meal.
- Ginger is an amazing source of phenolic compounds and provides great relief in gastrointestinal irritation. It also increases the saliva and bile production along with decreasing gastric contractions. Moreover, it facilitates the movement of food and fluids through the gastrointestinal tract.
- It is also known to treat nausea and vomiting. It is quite effective in reducing morning sickness as it is antiemetic in nature and is attributed with anti-flatulence properties as well. It is also effective in preventing seasickness or motion sickness.
- It is diaphoretic (capable of producing perspiration or sweating), thereby increasing the temperature of the body from within, resulting in comfort from extreme cold.
- Ginger is an antioxidant and helps fight oxidative stress, aka free radicals, and chronic inflammation. Due to this, it acts as an anti-ageing agent, too. The antioxidant property is the crucial player in reducing the chances of Alzheimer's in an individual. It also facilitates the proper functioning of the brain.
- Ginger is also beneficial for the smooth functioning of the heart. It has been seen that consuming ginger reduces the level of bad cholesterol (LDL), thus, lowering the possibility of heart diseases.

- It works towards boosting the immune system, preventing certain disorders like cough, cold, and throat irritation. It also prevents fatty accumulation in the arteries, thus, working wonders for the heart.
- Ginger also has pain-relieving qualities and has been clinically proven that it can reduce muscle spasms. Moreover, it also helps ease menstrual cramps.
- Gingerol in ginger is reported to display analgesic and powerful anti-inflammatory characteristics, which help in decreasing inflammation, pain, and swelling. Ginger is effective in anti-inflammatory conditions and provides a great sense of ease in dealing with two painful conditions—rheumatoid arthritis (a chronic ailment causing inflammation in the joints, resulting in painful deformities and immobility in fingers, feet, ankles, and wrists) and osteoarthritis (degeneration of joint cartilage, which causes stiffness and pain in hips, knees, and thumbs).
- Consuming ginger is quite effective in improving insulin sensitivity, reducing triglycerides and bad cholesterol. It helps in lowering the blood sugar levels and the possibility of developing diabetes. It has been proven that consuming 2 gm ginger per day can help control the blood sugar levels in the body.
- It also acts as an anti-cancer ingredient. It has great anti-carcinogenic properties, reducing the chances of cancers like breast cancer, colorectal cancer, skin cancer, liver, and bladder cancer. It has the power to induce apoptosis—death of cells to control organism growth—and stop the spread of cancer cells.

- It helps in effective absorption and stimulation of essential nutrients in the body as it secretes desired gastric and pancreatic enzymes.
- It is also used to control allergic reactions and to cure various respiratory illnesses.

Trivia

When ginger is heated, it dries due to dehydration and the gingerol present in it converts into shogaols. Shogaols are considered to be two times spicier than gingerol; hence, when ginger is cooked, it becomes more pungent in taste. In other words, gingerol is the main constituent of fresh ginger and shogaols in dried ginger. Gingerol is responsible for imparting distinct fragrance and flavour to ginger.

Nutritive Highlights

Ginger contains 335 calories in 100 gm. It also contains amino acids, raw fibres, protein, phytosterols, vitamins—vitamin A, vitamin C, niacin, and nicotinic acid—and minerals. The percentage of nutrient keeps changing in its various distinct forms like fresh ginger and dried form. It also consists of:

- 80 per cent moisture
- 50–70 per cent carbohydrate and dietary fibres
- 5 per cent protein
- 3–8 per cent lipids and terpenes—zingiberene, β-bisabolene, α-curcumene, etc., and phenolic compounds—gingerol, paradol and shogaol)

17
Curd

'One bit of advice someone gave me—which I haven't yet tried—is that if you go to an area where you might pick up a tummy bug, you should seek out the local probiotic yogurt. Eating it will introduce you to the local gut flora, apparently'

—Anthony Head

Curd, also known as yogurt, is a fermented food that is prepared by adding bacteria culture to the milk. The bacteria added—*Lactobacillus bulgaricus and Streptococcus thermophilus*—in the milk transforms its consistency, making it sour. The bacteria ferment the lactose present in milk and converts it into lactic acid. With an increase in the lactic acid, its pH level decreases, and the milk clots and achieves the texture of yogurt. This process is unique as it allows the milk's nutrients to last longer in the form of curd.

Commercially produced curd must contain, at least, 8.25 per cent solids and not fats. In commercial curd, stabilizers such as alginate, gelatine, pectin, and starch are added to provide better texture and firmness. Curd is a great example of probiotic food, which has endless benefits to humankind.

Curd is a probiotic food with several volatile composites like carbonyl compounds, alcohol, acid, ester, aromatic compounds, sulphur compounds, etc. The key flavour and aroma of curd is due to the presence of lactic acid, acetaldehyde, diacetyl, and acetone.

When it comes which product is more beneficial—milk or curd—then certain facts need to be highlighted. As far as calcium content is concerned, 100 gm of milk has 125 gm of calcium and 100 gm of curd consists of just 85 gm of calcium. But when compared to milk, curd is easier to digest, making it a great product for a lactose-intolerant individual. Moreover, it is exceptionally good for the digestive system as it cleanses it in an effective manner and avoids stomach and intestinal infections. Overall, curd, being probiotic in nature, is superior to milk.

Curd is a treasure trove of nutrients comprising proteins, vitamins, and minerals like vitamin D, vitamin B12, riboflavin, potassium, calcium, and zinc. Its incorporation can transform one's life for the better. It also has great anti-ageing properties and is beneficial for the heart, liver, skin, and hair.

Below are some more qualities of curd:

- Curd is rich in nutrients that have plenty of trace minerals and vitamins like calcium, vitamin B12, riboflavin, phosphorus, magnesium, potassium, and vitamin D. Each nutrient plays a specific role in maintaining good health and is beneficial for those suffering from micronutrient deficiency.
- Curd is an exemplary probiotic food, which is why it is different from all the other food products. The advantages of probiotic food is not hidden from anyone as it keeps the gut in check. A healthy gut improves the overall immunity of an individual and improves the digestive system, keeping constipation, bloating,

and flatulence at bay. Moreover, it is beneficial to those who are lactose intolerant as well.

- Along with improving one's immunity, its consumption also reduces the chances of various vaginal infections as it balances the pH value.
- By improving digestion, curd has also proven its worth in cases of diarrhoea and any ailments associated with the stomach or gastrointestinal tract. Curd is also advised to those experiencing dysentery as it has the power to stabilise the pH level, facilitating powerful digestion.
- Calcium and phosphorus are found in abundance in curd and both the minerals are extremely helpful in boosting the health of bones, in turn, improving bone density. It helps in avoiding disease like arthritis and osteoporosis.
- Curd is a rich source of minerals like magnesium and potassium, which is effective in lowering one's blood pressure by balancing the harmful effects of salt. High blood pressure can put an individual's heart at risk; thus, curd plays a key role in managing one's cardiovascular activities.
- The daily intake of curd is also effective in the formation of cholesterol, specifically in the arterial region, making it useful in preventing hypertension.
- Curd is loaded with abundance of calcium. Calcium can restrict the formation of cortisol—a hormone that is active in metabolism of carbohydrate and protein. Cortisol formation leads to an increase in weight. Consuming curd increases the production of appetite-reducing hormones like peptide YY and GLP-1

(glucagon-like peptide). Thus, making curd a regular part of the diet can help in maintaining weight, too.

- Casein is the chief constituent of curd, which is the protein of milk and is responsible for imparting curd its white colour. It is high in protein—about 10–12 per cent, depending on the milk being used. Due to its protein content, it is rich in amino acids like methionine, which protects the liver from getting fat, ensuring better liver health.

  Other sources of methionine are: Eggs, meat, fish, and sesame seeds.

- Curd is a rich source of vitamin E and zinc, and these components make it an ideal ingredient for good skin. Vitamin E and zinc are responsible for a glowing skin, making it to absorb optimum nutrients. It firms up the skin and prevents acne, too. Curd is also used as an ingredient in several skincare products.

- Lactic acid is an important ingredient of curd as it provides nutrients and minerals that are required by the scalp to fight dandruff, dull hair, and other such problems associated with hair. Thus, both the external application and its consumption are beneficial for good hair.

- Curd is one of the best foods in whetting the appetite. People who are advised to eat more or suffer from anorexia nervosa are asked to make curd a part of their diet.

Nutritive Highlights

The nutritional ratio of curd keeps changing on the kind of milk used depending upon the animal milk is sourced from, and whether one is using skimmed or toned milk. It is also a source of vitamin A, vitamin D, vitamin B12, sodium, potassium, and magnesium. It consists of:

- 88 per cent water
- 98 calories in 100 gm
- 9 gm protein
- 3.4 gm carbohydrate
- 4.3 gm fat in 100 gm of curd

18
Turmeric

'I'm just keeping the faith. I continue to eat well, take turmeric, cayenne pepper, milk and honey, and exercise my eye muscles frequently.'
—Traci Medford-Rosow

Turmeric is a rhizome from the ginger family, Zingiberaceae. It can be used fresh or in dried form. After drying, it attains a deep orange yellow colour and is powdered and used as a spice. When harvested, turmeric's root is boiled, cleaned, cured, dried, and then grounded to get the yellow spice powder. It is known for its bitter and earthy flavour and is used for colouring various delicacies. It is also used by the cosmetic industry.

Turmeric has two chief components: Turmerone (volatile oil) and curcuminoid (colouring agent). Curcumin, the bioactive compound, is the significant constituent of curcuminoids and is considered to be a natural antioxidant. This curcuminoid is the principal ingredient in turmeric, which has several benefits and makes turmeric so special. Curcumin in turmeric is present in small amount, around 5–7 per cent, but its benefits are magnificent.

Turmeric can be used in multiple ways as a culinary spice ingredient, medicinal constituent, and in the cosmetic and skincare industry as well. Its worth is as golden as its appearance.

Some more features of turmeric are:

- Turmeric is a potent antioxidant that has dominant anti-inflammatory properties. Chronic inflammation, if persisting for long, results in inflammatory bowel ailments, pancreatitis, and arthritis. But regular intake of turmeric helps in preventing such diseases and provides relief from them, too.

  According to one study, curcumin is so powerful an anti-inflammatory that medications used for inflammatory conditions are also less effective compared to it.
- Turmeric has anti-cancer properties; hence, its intake reduces cell proliferation and induces apoptosis, programmed death of cancer cells. As curcumin, which is present in turmeric, is a powerful anti-inflammatory, it restricts the growth of tumour, restricting the risk of colorectal, pancreatic, breast, gastric, and prostate cancer. It disrupts the formation of cancerous cells interfering with cell-signalling pathways and even kills these cancerous cells. Thus, curcumin is a great anti-carcinogen.
- Turmeric also acts as a mighty digestive stimulant as its consumption can improve the functioning of pancreatic lipase and stimulate bile secretion. Its intake increases the production of digestive juices, thereby improving digestion.
- Curcumin improves the endothelium and its function. Endothelium is the tissue that forms the single layer of cells in various organs, especially blood vessels and heart, and is significant in the regulation of blood

pressure. When its efficiency decreases, the possibility of heart diseases increases, but curcumin improves the endothelial function, decreasing the possibility of heart diseases. It is so impactful that its regular consumption equals the benefits of aerobic exercises spanning over eight months. It also lowers the level of bad cholesterol (LDL) to a great extent, which is good for cardiovascular health.

- Curcumin also helps in lowering blood sugar along with increasing plasma insulin, thereby treating and preventing diabetes. Its anti-inflammatory and antioxidant characteristic result in the resistance towards insulin, high blood sugar, and hyperlipidaemia (an unusual high concentration of fats or lipids in the bloodstream).
- Curcumin is versatile in its effects and is useful in the treatment of osteoarthritis— degeneration of joint cartilage and underlying bone resulting in pain and stiffness mainly in knee, hip and thumb joints. Those who suffer from this disease have displayed tremendous improvement when treated with a dose of natural curcuminoid mixture which consists of 75 per cent curcumin, 15 per cent desmethoxycurcumin, and 10 per cent bisdemethoxycurcumin.
- Curcumin is also effective in keeping the special protein available in brain and spinal cord, which plays a significant role in keeping the nerve cells healthy along with regulation between nerve cells. Curcumin magnifies the level of brain-derived neurotrophic factor (BDNF), which is great for brain health. This improves learning and memory and reverses brain degeneration as well. Thus, turmeric is a key player in treating and delaying Alzheimer's.

- Alzheimer's leads to depression due to the reduced levels of BDNF in the body. Turmeric, due to its curcumin content, is capable of increasing BDNF levels, thus, acting as an antidepressant.
- Research has proven that curcumin is also capable of protecting the eyes from degeneration and preventing glaucoma (damage of the optic nerve), which may lead to blindness in the elderly.
- Intake of curcumin, through turmeric, is also helpful in treating painful conditions due to rheumatoid arthritis.
- Gifted with antimicrobial properties, turmeric is used effectively in treating skin conditions like acne, eczema, psoriasis, and photoaging (skin damage due to long sun exposure and ultraviolet radiations).
- Turmeric is used to treat various wounds and protects us against infections in general.
- Turmeric is a potent antioxidant, and it is known to be effective in preventing the premature signs of ageing. Its consumption results in one's longevity by fighting free radicals, thus, resulting in good health of an individual.
- The volatile oil from turmeric is also used for treating respiratory tract disorders. It actually helps in removing sputum—a mixture of saliva and mucous blocking the respiratory tract, providing relief from cough and avoiding asthma.
- Volatile turmeric oil also keeps mosquitoes at bay.

Trivia

Turmeric obtains its aroma from components like turmerone, arturmerone, and zingiberene. Its plant does not propagate by means of seed but by underground rhizomes.

Nutritive Highlights

Turmeric contains 390 calories in 100 gm. It is loaded with vitamin C, Vitamin E, vitamin K, thiamine, riboflavin, betaine, and choline. It also contains calcium, magnesium, potassium, phosphorus, sodium, copper, iron, selenium, and zinc. It is a rich source of Omega-3 fatty acids and α-linolenic. It consists of:

- 65 per cent carbohydrate
- 1/3rd dietary fibre of carbohydrate
- 7.85 per cent protein
- 1 per cent fat
- 6 per cent ash content
- 11 per cent moisture
- 10 gm of total fat
- 0.26 gm phosphorus
- 10 mg potassium
- 47.5 mg iron

19
Fish

'It's okay to eat fish because they don't have any feelings.'

—Kurt Cobain

Fish is, undoubtedly, the best and healthiest food offered to humankind as it is high in protein and low in fat. In India, there is a segment of population that considers fish as the 'Fruits of the Sea', and they abstain from eating meat and egg but consume fish with great gusto. They are also known as pescatarians.

Fish is a prominent source of various nutrients across the globe. It is divided into various categories like oily fish, fatty fish, round fish, etc., and this distinct quality of fish has distinct nutritional value, structure, and usage. It is so versatile in the culinary world that it would be hard to resist it, at least, by those who are concerned about its nutritional values and benefits offered to human beings.

Some more features of this superfood are listed below:

- Fish is an excellent source of nutrients like Omega-3 fatty acids that play a prominent role in maintaining optimum health of the brain. It has been found to lower the risk of several diseases. It provides fat-soluble vitamins like vitamin D. It is also a rich source of protein and few minerals.

- Fish is also good for those who are at the risk of brain diseases like Alzheimer's. It improves the control on one's emotions along with improving memory. Fish intake avoids cerebral atrophy and deterioration.
- Omega-3 fatty acids are ample in fatty fish. It has been observed that the regular consumption of fish, especially fatty fish, lowers the chances of heart attacks and strokes, which are some of the prime reasons behind premature deaths.
- Docosahexaenoic acid (DHA), an Omega-3 fatty acid, is found in abundance in fish and is required for the proper growth and development of human beings. The Omega-3 fatty acid is associated with impeccable brain functioning and is beneficial for the eyes as well. Expecting and breastfeeding women are advised to take Omega-3 fatty acids to obtain optimum benefits.
- Omega-3 fatty acids, present in fish, have been seen as an effective antidepressant. It is also beneficial in conditions like bipolar disorder—a mental disorder that is marked by alternating periods of exhilaration and depression.
- Omega-3 fatty acids are helpful in autoimmune diseases like diabetes. It builds and boosts the immune system so that the attacks on the tissues are incapable to take the shape of diabetes.
- It has been clinically proven that consuming fish once a week can decrease the chances of macular degeneration in the elderly.

- The deficiency of vitamin D is quite common and is increasing at an alarming rate. This gap can be bridged by the consumption of fish as they are a good source of vitamin D. Certain fish like cod liver, salmon, and herring are excellent sources of vitamin D.
- People who consume fish frequently are less prone to digestive cancers such as colon cancer, pancreatic cancer, pharynx cancer, etc., as compared to someone eating fish once in a while.
- It has been found in the study of Academy of Nutrition and Dietetics that students who consume fatty fish as compared to red meat have a higher concentration level as it helps in improving concentration in teenagers.
- Fish is highly effective in breaking down triglycerides and fatty acids in the liver, thereby decreasing the possibility of a fatty liver.
- The Omega-3 fatty acids found in fish have also been helpful in decreasing the bad cholesterol level and increasing the good cholesterols. The decrease in bad cholesterol and increase in good cholesterol has been effective in lowering the possibility of heart diseases like heart attack and stroke.
- Insomnia and poor sleep are due to either an excessive exposure of blue light or the deficiency of vitamin D. As fish is an excellent source of vitamin D, it helps in reducing sleep-related problems.
- Due to the presence of Omega-3, consuming fish keeps the blood platelets from forming a mass, thus, preventing the formation of harmful blood clots.

- People suffering from acne and other skin disorders have experienced better results with fish intake. Fish oil has been significant in clearing one's skin, making it glow.
- Asthmatic conditions can significantly reduce by the consumption of fish, especially in children.
- A regular intake of fish also helps in reducing the problems that arise with rheumatoid arthritis.

***Note:** Certain fish contain mercury, which is detrimental to brain health. Thus, pregnant women are advised to consume fish that are low in mercury; for instance, trout, sardines, and salmon. The possibility of consuming contaminated fish is also quite common due to improper practices by various industries. Hence, the chances of infections by consuming such fish are also high.*

Nutritive Highlights

Fish are available in wide variety of species with distinct nutritional compositions. Due to this, it is quite impossible to state the exact nutritional composition of fish. Nutrients like vitamins, carbohydrates, and other non-protein nitrogenous compounds are present in negligible amount but are of due significance. Fish are a rich source of desired nutrients like Omega-3 fatty acids and vitamin D. They are also a rich source of amino acids like lysine and methionine. The four main nutrients or constituents of fish are water, protein, lipid (or fat), and minerals (ash). In general, fish has around (the mentioned ratio may vary depending on the distinct composition of wide variety of fish):

- 65–90 per cent water
- 10–24 per cent protein
- The proteins in fish are classified into three major categories:
    - Sarcoplasmic protein—myogen and globulin are around 25–30 per cent of the total protein
    - Myofibrillar protein—actin, myosin, actomyosin, etc., and is around 65 per cent of muscle proteins
    - Stroma protein—collagen, etc.—and is around 10 per cent of the total protein component.
- 1–20 per cent fat
- 0.5–5 per cent mineral content
- 1–2 per cent carbohydrate

20
Eggs

'If you've broken the eggs, you should make the omelette.'
—Anthony Eden

Egg is the most versatile food on this planet as it can be prepared through various methods. The cherry on the top is that it is extremely nutritious and inexpensive and is packed with most essential nutrients needed by the human body. Eggs of birds like quail, duck, and chicken are consumed, but, in general, egg refers to a chicken's egg. The most crucial aspect associated with egg is that it is highly valued and is considered as a complete source of protein as it contains all the nine essential amino acids—Valine, leucine, threonine, histidine, tryptophan, phenylalanine, lysine, isoleucine, and methionine. These amino acids are not formed in our bodies; hence, the only source is including them in our diet.

Some features and benefits of eggs are:

- Egg is an excellent source of choline (vitamin B-complex family). It is beneficial in stimulating and rejuvenating brain health by keeping memory, mood, and emotion in a healthy state. It is also helpful in regulating muscle control and keeping the liver free from fat content and certain diseases—like cardiovascular ailments and dementia—at bay. Thus, egg is considered one of the healthiest foods.

- Choline intake in pregnant women has been found to improve the brain development of the foetus and is associated with cognitive development in children in later stages as well.

  Other sources of choline are: Mushroom, liver, salmon, beans, legumes, and cruciferous vegetables.

- Eating eggs provides one with a feeling of satiety for a longer period. Thus, egg is much better for those who are aiming to lose some weight.

- Egg is an excellent source of carotenoids and is accountable for boosting the immune system when consumed regularly. The yellow colour of the yolk is due to the presence of xanthophylls. Lutein and zeaxanthin are crucial for better eye health and the cognitive understanding of the brain in both children and adults. They also help in preventing cataract and macular degeneration. Egg contains fatty acids due to which the xanthophylls are easily absorbed and digested by the body.

  Moreover, vitamin A is also present in the egg, making it significant for improving one's eye health.

- Egg contains vitamin D, which facilitates the proper absorption of calcium, thereby improving bone health and aiding neuromuscular—related to the nerves and muscles—functions. It also decreases inflammation.

- The trace minerals in an egg like iodine and selenium are ample, and they are crucial for the development of the brain and improving thyroid and liver functions. Thus, egg intake improves conditions like thyroid and fatty liver.

- Egg is also rich in Omega-3 fatty acids, especially docosahexaenoic acid (DHA), and this DHA is responsible for the proper functioning of the brain, improving vision, and lowering triglyceride level.
  Other sources of DHA are: Fish
- Egg is, indeed, a food rich in cholesterol. It increases good cholesterol and reduces the bad cholesterol. It has been studied that few people are hyper responders to the consumption of eggs, and in such people, eggs may increase the LDL and the total cholesterol level. Thus, normally eating egg is helpful for promoting good cardiovascular health.
- Egg provides ample protein. It is believed that one large egg provides around 6 gm of protein. This protein consumption results in weight loss and an increase in muscle mass. It also optimises bone health and lowers blood pressure. Protein present in egg is, in fact, a complete protein.

***Note:** A glycoprotein called avidin is present in raw egg. Avidin combines with vitamin B-complex biotin, and this complex combination of avidin-biotin is not absorbed by our digestive tract. Hence, consuming raw eggs can lead to a biotin deficiency.*

Trivia

'Biological Value' (BV) is a term that is used for the quality of protein, measuring the rate of efficiency about protein used for growth. Eggs top the list on an efficiency scale of 100 with 93.7 BV, fish 76.0 BV, beef 74.3 BV, soybeans 72.8 BV, rice and wheat 64BV, corn 60.0, and dried beans 58.0 BV. Thus, it is apparent that eggs are indeed an excellent source of quality protein.

Nutritive Highlights

Eggs are an excellent source of Omega-3 fatty acids, choline, potassium, phosphorus, magnesium, calcium, iron, and fat-soluble vitamins like Vitamin A, D, E, and K).

- 1 medium-sized boiled egg yields 84 calories
- 8.3 gm of protein
- 5.7 gm of fat
- 1.6 gm of saturated fat
- 87 per cent water
- 13 per cent protein, along with vitamin and minerals

Egg yolk contains around:

- 50 per cent water
- 17 per cent protein
- 33 per cent fat

(Egg yolk contains around 40 per cent protein, 10 per cent vitamin B3, 38 per cent vitamin B2, 90 per cent of the total egg fat, 70 per cent manganese, 75 per cent vitamin B1, 80 per cent biotin (vitamin B7 or B8), and 59 per cent selenium of the entire egg nutrition.)

Egg white consists of:

- 60 per cent protein
- 90 per cent vitamin B3

- 62 per cent vitamin B2
- 10 per cent total egg fat
- 30 per cent manganese
- 25 per cent vitamin B1
- 20 per cent biotin
- 41 per cent selenium

21
Mushrooms

'Advice is like mushrooms. The wrong kind can prove fatal.'
—Charles E. McKenzie

Mushroom is the fleshy, spore-bearing fruiting body of a fungus. It can be grown on the soil or on its food source. Nonetheless, it is classified as a vegetable, but it belongs to a fungi family and not a plant group. The white button mushroom is the most common variety of edible mushrooms and is generally referred to as 'mushroom'. It is available in wide varieties and they all have their own significance in the culinary and nutritive worlds. Few varieties are toxic or poisonous and should be avoided as it is difficult to distinguish edible mushrooms from toxic ones.

Mushrooms have been used in a wide variety of delicacies and are acknowledged for its super nutritive value by all. The common edible varieties present in the mushroom family are Agaricus (white mushrooms), crimini (brown mushrooms), portabella (largest mushrooms), chanterelle (funnel-shaped mushroom), shiitake (umbrella-shaped, thin-stemmed mushrooms), oyster (oyster-shaped, delicate mushrooms), enoki (smallest mushroom), porcini (reddish-brown cap with a thick stem), morels (sweet, earthy mushrooms), and truffle (most valued mushrooms).

Below are some more features and benefits of mushrooms:

- Mushroom is packed with two antioxidant compounds—glutathione and ergothioneine. Both the antioxidants present in mushrooms are beneficial in preventing neurodegenerative diseases (disease associated with the central nervous system and leads to the death of certain brain parts) like Parkinson's— brain disorder associated with shaking, stiffness, improper balance, and lack of coordination, and Alzheimer's. Mushrooms bolster the immune system and enable one to fight various free radicals in the body.

  Note: *Glutathione is present in porcini mushrooms, whereas ergothioneine is present in oyster mushrooms. The percentage of both antioxidants varies tremendously in different varieties of mushrooms.*

  Other sources of glutathione are: Brussels sprout, cabbage, spinach, broccoli, garlic, chives, tomatoes, asparagus, almonds, cucumber, and walnuts.

  Other sources of ergothioneine are: Black beans, kidney beans, oat bran, and liver and kidney of chicken and lamb.

- Mushroom is respected for its low-calorie and fibre-rich content. It is loaded with several significant vitamins and minerals. The fibre present in abundance in mushrooms is accountable for reducing the cholesterol levels in the body, along with promoting a strong immune system.

- Mushroom is of extreme value due to the presence of antioxidants, polyphenols, polysaccharides, selenium, and vitamin C. All these nutrients enable it to combat cancer cells. Selenium present in mushrooms help fight these cancer cells. The unique polysaccharides called beta-glucans—sugar found in cell walls of bacteria, yeast, and fungi—are capable of improving the immune system by activating macrophages—large white blood cells that eat harmful particles like bacteria, viruses, and parasites in the body and are a crucial part of the immune system—and natural killer cells. It protects one from various infections as well.

Other sources of beta-glucans are: Oats, barley, whole grain, and algae.

- Mushrooms have certain phenolic group compounds—like flavonoids and phenolic acids—present in it that are also blessed with antioxidant characteristics. Due to its function, it restricts the growth of tumours and kills cancer cells.
  Note: *The chief dietary phenolic compounds are phenolic acids, flavonoids and tannins. All such compounds are antioxidant in nature, hence, play a significant role in reducing lipid oxidation in plant and animal tissues. Due to this, it conserves food for a longer duration, thereby improving the quality of food it is added to. It also decreases the possibility of several diseases like cancer, diabetes, cardiovascular diseases, and neurological disorders.*
- Mushroom is produced in farms with enough exposure to sunlight, making it a natural source of vitamin D2, also known as ergocalciferol. This vitamin D2 is converted into vitamin D. Vitamin D is responsible for facilitating calcium absorption in the body and maintaining healthy bones. Thus, including mushrooms in your diet can prevent bone-related conditions like osteoporosis.

Note: Mushroom is the only plant food which contains vitamin D.

- Mushroom also takes care of the smooth functioning of the heart. The ergothioneines present in it is capable of reducing inflammation, fighting free radicals, and lowering the cholesterol and triglycerides levels. Ergothioneine also restricts the possibility of plaque formation in the arteries.

  Note: *The plaque in the arteries is made up of fat particles, cholesterol, calcium, and few other substances. With the passage of time, plaque gets stuck to the walls of the artery and becomes firm, causing blockage. Due to this blockage, the blood flow is restricted to many parts of the body. This condition is called atherosclerosis.*

- Mushroom is rich in polysaccharides, which help in lowering the blood sugar level and improving the resistance towards insulin. Polysaccharides functions as a prebiotic as well, making it beneficial for gut flora. It acts as the feed for gut bacteria, promoting good gut health.
- Selenium is a mineral found in mushrooms, which plays a key role in the proper functioning of the liver by secreting enough enzymes. It also acts as a detoxifying agent by tossing cancer-related compounds out of the body. Selenium is a great anti-inflammatory as well and lowers the risk of tumour growth.

  Other sources of selenium are: Fish, ham, pork, chicken, beef, spinach, jaggery, bananas, oats, egg, and lentils.

- Selenium also kills Malassezia—a genus of fungi found on skin surfaces—on the scalp. These fungi lead to shedding dry skin fragments and selenium helps in improving this condition while improving hair growth and preventing dandruff as well.

- Mushroom has a good amount of potassium and negligible amount of sodium, which makes it beneficial in maintaining one's blood pressure. Thus, mushroom intake accounts for perfect cardiovascular functions.
- Mushroom contains two dietary fibres—beta-glucans and chitin. Both give a feeling of satiety, decreasing the appetite, which, in turn, results in lower consumption of food and overall calorie intake.

  Note: *Chitin is a fibrous substance from polysaccharides and is a part of cell walls of fungi.*

  Other sources of chitin are: Crustaceans (crab, shrimp, and lobster) and waste of fish industry.
- Mushrooms are a source of choline, which helps sooth the mind. It promotes quality sleep, cognitive learning, and improves memory. It also improves the structure of cell membranes and decreases chronic inflammation.
- Mushroom contains lectins—a class of proteins, especially of plant origin—which binds with the cancer cells and destroys them. It has been clinically seen that mushrooms fight breast cancer, liver cancer, gastric cancer, pancreatic cancer, and uterine cervix cancer.

  Other sources of lectins are: Peanuts, lentils, tomatoes, potatoes, eggplant, fruits, and wheat and other grains.

Nutritive Highlights

Mushroom is a rich source of riboflavin (vitamin B2), niacin (vitamin B3), pantothenic acid (vitamin B5), vitamin D, selenium, phosphorus, zinc, and folate (vitamin B9). It also consists of:

- 90 per cent water (water content varies slightly from 88 to 92 per cent depending upon the variety of the mushroom)
- 21 calories in 100 gm
- 2–3 per cent protein
- 3–4 per cent carbohydrate

22
Almonds

'I like almonds as a snack—keeps your energy up but doesn't fill you up.'
—Ina Garten

Almonds are the edible seeds of Prunus dulcis, also known as the almond tree. They are quite expensive as compared to other variety of nuts. They are subtly flavoured but crunchy in nature and have great nutritive values. Few varieties of almonds are easily available in the market like mamra almond, Californian almond, etc. These light brown nuts are used in many sweet dishes to add new dimension in terms of taste, flavour, garnish, and boost the nutritive value as well.

The skin of almonds is rich in antioxidants. Polyphenols and prebiotic fibre have the maximum quantity of phenolic compounds like flavonols—kaempferol, quercetin, catechin, and epicatechin; flavanones—naringenin; anthocyanins—cyanidins; and phenolic acids—caffeic acid, ferulic acid, etc., present in it. Almonds consist of simple proteins like globulins—amandine and albumin—and amino acids like arginine, histidine, lysine, valine, methionine, cystine, leucine, etc. All these compounds add to the benefits delivered by almonds.

Features and benefits of almonds are:

- Almonds are the only high-fat foods that are healthy to consume on a regular basis. They are rich in monounsaturated fats, which are responsible for increasing good cholesterol and decreasing the bad cholesterol. LDL is associated with ailments like atherosclerosis and heart attack. Thus, almonds lower the risk of heart attacks.
- Almond has the unique quality to reduce the after-meal blood sugar level. This protects one from diabetes and cardiovascular diseases. Almonds also reduce the cholesterol-damaging free radicals linked with blood sugar elevations. Thus, almond effectively controls diabetes as well.
- Two trace minerals—manganese and copper—are adequately present in almonds. Both the minerals are cofactors, i.e. works favourably together, to very crucial oxidative enzyme, superoxide dismutase. Together, it controls the harmful free radicals that are generated inside the mitochondria, resulting in proper energy flow.
- Riboflavin is also present in adequate amount in almonds, which plays a prominent role in the energy production. Riboflavin produces two biomolecules, flavin adenine dinucleotide (FAD) or flavin mononucleotide (FMN), which are flavoproteins that contain nucleic acid derivative of riboflavin. This flavoprotein functions towards the energy production in the body. Thus, riboflavin is crucial in the body's smooth functioning.
- Almond is also a rich source of vitamin E and has antioxidant properties as well. Thus, it fights with the

free radicals and prevents our body from their harmful effects. It also protects us from the sun burn, and its consumption results in good cardiovascular health. It is also necessary for avoiding any symptoms of cognitive decline and boosting memory and alertness.

- An excellent source of nutrients such as vitamin E, calcium, magnesium, and potassium, the combination of all these nutrients is extremely essential in promoting the testosterone level in men. Thus, almond plays a chief role in boosting the libido and acts as aphrodisiac as well.
- Almond is gluten-free and packed with dense nutrients like fibre, vitamin B, and protein. Normally, a gluten-free diet lacks such nutrients and almond is a great source to bridge this gap and is highly recommended for anyone on a gluten-free diet.
- As almond has been scaled with lower GI, its consumption leads to decrease the meal's glycaemic index and thereby control the fall and rise of sugar blood levels to minimal scale. Thus, it has been very beneficial for the people suffering from diabetes.
- Almond is loaded with sufficient quantities of fat and fibre, and both these nutrients prohibit the formation of gallstones and allow the liver and gallbladder to function extremely smoothly.
- Almonds also aid in weight loss. So, munching on almonds as compared to any other high-carb food is more beneficial.
- The brain health of an individual is taken care of by nutrients like vitamin E, folate, unsaturated fatty acids, and L-carnitine present in almonds.

Note: L-carnitine is a derivative of amino acids—lysine and methionine—and it aids in transporting fatty acids into the cells to produce energy.

- The alpha-tocopherol present in almonds acts as a photoprotectant (biochemical process that aids organisms to deal with damage done by sunlight) and is used to treat and cure skin ailments like psoriasis and eczema. It prevents our skin from harmful rays.
- Vitamin E present in almond also boosts the health of one's hair. Its deficiency causes hair loss and thinning. Moreover, it helps improve the strength of nails.
- Almond is loaded with tocopherol, folate, polyphenols, and monounsaturated fatty acids, and they help in preventing the genesis of cognitive disorders and amnesia.

Note: *Glycaemic Index (GI) is a rating criterion, which rates carbohydrate foods by their impact on blood sugar levels in comparison with the absorption of 50 gm of glucose (reference food in this matter), containing the GI value of 100. The assigned value of GI is: Low GI value—55 or less, medium GI value—56–69, and high GI value—70 or more. Food with a low GI is the most preferred as it is gradually digested and absorbed, leading to a minor rise in blood sugar levels. Intake of food with a high GI must be limited as it is instantly digested and absorbed with intense rise and fall in the blood sugar levels. Lastly, carbohydrate-rich food can only be defined with its GI value.*

Nutritive Highlights

Almonds are high in fat, rich in monounsaturated fatty acids and fibre. They contain folate (vitamin B9), biotin, vitamin E, vitamin B2, phosphorus, selenium, magnesium, molybdenum, copper, etc., in abundance. It also consists of:

- 550 calories in 100 gm
- 22 gm protein in 100 gm
- 50 gm fat (of which 62 per cent comprises the most beneficial monounsaturated Omega-9 fatty acids, i.e. oleic acid; 24 per cent polyunsaturated Omega-6 fatty acid, i.e. linoleic acid; and 6 per cent saturated fatty acid, i.e. palmitic acid)
- 19 gm carbohydrate in a 100 gm
- 60 per cent dietary fibre
- 20 per cent fructose

23

Spinach

'Leafy greens such as romaine lettuce, kale, collards, Swiss chard, and spinach are the most nutrient-dense of all foods.'

—Joel Fuhrman

Spinach, a member of the amaranth family, is a leafy vegetable that is consumed fresh, preserved, cooked, or raw and has distinct taste. Spinach leaves vary in size and are green in colour due to the presence of chlorophyll. Spinach is a fast-growing crop which is highly sensitive to heat and is grown during winters. It is easy to cook and is acknowledged for its stupendous nutritional significance.

It is recommended to store spinach in your refrigerator as the nutrients present in it, like vitamin C, vitamin B6, and carotenoids, are destroyed because of heat. And refrigerating spinach retains its nutrients for a longer period.

Some of the qualities of spinach are:

- Spinach is a rich source of phytonutrients like glucuronide and glucopyranonside, which are associated with the flavonoids forms of spinacetin, patuletin, and jaceidin. All these compounds have remarkable anti-inflammatory properties.

- Spinach is also a rich source of carotenoids (of the group epoxyxanthophylls) like lutein, zeaxanthin, neoxanthin, and violaxanthin. All these carotenoids are powerful anti-inflammatories.
- Spinach is low in fat content but is exceptionally high in nutrients like Omega-3 fatty acids and diacyglycerols, which contains eicosapentaenoic acid (EPA). The Omega-3 fatty acids are also remarkable in treating anti-inflammatory symptoms.
- Chlorophyll and thylakoid are present in spinach, and they aid in regulating hunger, provide satiety, and maintain the blood sugar levels as well. The consumption of spinach is effective in decreasing the hunger-related hormones like ghrelin, thus, increasing the level of satiety-associated hormones like glucagon-like peptide 1 (GLP-1). This aids in weight loss.
- Spinach is an excellent source of fibre. It stimulates the digestive system and adds bulk to the stool as food passes through the digestive system. It provides a great relief in those who suffer from constipation.
- A splendid source of vitamin C, vitamin K, folic acid, iron, and calcium, spinach is beneficial for good skin, too. Moreover, it helps in blood clotting and is essential for boosting cellular function and tissue growth in pregnant women. It aids in the formation of haemoglobin, supplying oxygen to the tissues, and boosting bone health.
- Spinach consists of sufficient vitamin A and compounds like lutein and zeaxanthin. These nutrients are helpful for one's eye health, thus, improving vision. It also prevents macular degeneration and cataract.

- Spinach contains nitrate, which has the capability of regulating one's blood pressure, in so doing, decreasing the possibility of heart diseases.

Note:

- *It has been proven that spinach experiences 25 per cent of folate loss and a substantial loss of vitamin C as well when it is microwaved and boiled rather than steamed. The loss of carotenoid can be minimised by sautéing the spinach instead of frying, boiling, or steaming. This loss occurs because it contains water- and fat-soluble vitamins in abundance. This has been found in the study conducted by Human Nutrition Research Center on Aging at Tufts University.*
- *The nitrate incorporated in food additives are not considered good for one's health. Spinach also contains nitrate, but its content is less than 1 milligram per ounces; hence, it is considered beneficial for the human body as it is converted from nitrate to nitrite or nitric oxide—the chief component that aids in the functioning of the intestinal lining. But this fact regarding nitrate content and its benefits are still being researched.*
- *Spinach attains it green colour due to the pigment called chlorophyll, and this pigment is stored in chloroplasts inside the plants. Their membranes play a significant role in converting sunlight into energy, which is known as photosynthesis. The chloroplast-related membranes are called thylakoids, which is associated with reducing hunger-related hormones like ghrelin, increasing satiety.*
- *Spinach consists of calcium and oxalates (naturally occurring organic acids), and they combine to form calcium*

oxalate. The formation of calcium oxalate adds to the risk of formation of kidney stones. Hence, anyone prone to kidney stones should refrain from eating spinach.

- *Vitamin K present in spinach is capable of clotting the blood, hence anyone on blood-thinning medications must avoid spinach.*

Nutritive Highlights

Spinach is extremely low in calorie with just 23 calories in 100 gm. It is an excellent source of vitamin K, vitamin A, vitamin B2, Vitamin B6, manganese, magnesium, folate, iron, copper, phosphorus, Vitamin C, pantothenic acid, Vitamin E, choline, selenium, and Omega-3 fatty acids. It also comprises numerous antioxidant compounds of flavonoids like spinacetin, patuletin, and jaceidin and carotenoid compounds like lutein, neoxanthin, and violaxanthin. It is also rich in fibre.

Spinach also consists of:

- 91 per cent water
- 3 per cent protein
- 3.6 per cent carbohydrate
- less than 0.5 per cent fat

24
WALNUTS

'The world leaders should eat a walnut daily for the world peace; therefore, it plays remarkably healthy, for the mental health.'

—Ehsan Sehgal

Walnut is a nut or an edible seed of a drupe. It belongs to the genus Juglans, aka walnut trees. It is a single-seed fruit, and its meat kernel is used after it has ripened properly. The shell is discarded and the seed is consumed. The shelled walnut kernels are a rich source of antioxidants. In fact, its oil is rather expensive. The walnut kernel resembles the structure of human brain and is considered beneficial for brain health.

Below are some of the characteristics of walnuts:

- Walnut is packed with bioactive compounds like phytosterols, gamma-tocopherol, Omega-3 fatty acids, ellagic acid, and many other polyphenols. All these compounds are known to restrict the abnormal growth of cancerous cells and reduce the possibility of colon and prostate cancers.
- Walnut is effective in decreasing the risk of various cardiovascular issues. It is capable of reducing bad

cholesterol and inflammation. It also improves the blood vessel functions and prohibits the formation of plaque in the arteries.

- Proteins are found in abundance in walnuts, and it is no hidden secret that protein aids in rebuilding the tissues in our body. It also stimulates the feeling of satiety. Walnut contains several essential amino acids that are required by our body for physiological processes like muscle repair and its maintenance.
- It is a great vegan source of Omega-3 fatty acids. Walnut comprises alpha-linoleic acid (ALA), which is converted into DHA and EPA. Thus, walnuts must be consumed to derive the optimum benefits.
- Walnut is also composed of melatonin—a hormone secreted by the pineal gland—which is a messaging molecule, working towards better and sound sleep and light-dark adjustment. Melatonin is also believed to show anti-cancer properties.
- Metabolic syndrome is a condition that is associated with the surplus of blood fats (triglycerides), high blood pressure, and lower level of good cholesterol, and obesity. Aside from a large waist circumference, it increases the chances of heart attacks and other issues. The intake of walnut is found beneficial in reducing abdominal fat, thus, decreasing waist circumference as well.
- The fibre in walnut is also efficient in maintaining gastrointestinal regularity, promoting proper balance of blood sugar levels, and balancing healthy cholesterol.
- The potassium- and calcium-rich walnut is also helpful in maintaining the structural element of bones and cellular membranes. When both the nutrients are

consumed, they stimulate the formation of stronger bones and teeth.

- Walnuts, being rich in Omega-3 fatty acids, work superbly for brain health as our brain comprises structural fats that are essential for the normal functioning of brain cells. A low supply of Omega-3 fatty acids in children can result in learning disorders, behavioural problems, or increased possibilities of hyperactive mode.
- Walnut is capable of bolstering the immune system tremendously. The various components and antioxidants present in it work towards boosting one's immunity.
- Gallic acid is also in abundance in walnuts. It has powerful anti-fungal and anti-viral functions. It aids in protecting the cells from the harmful effects of free radicals. Gallic acid is also helpful in treating haemorrhage. It also cures ailments like diabetes and albuminuria (a kind of kidney disease wherein an excess of albumin is present in one's urine).

Note: *Walnut kernel skin consists of 90 per cent of phenols like phenolic acids, tannins, and flavonoids. Thus, it is not advisable to remove the whitish, waxy and flaky skin of the kernel.*

Nutritive Highlights

Walnut is rich in calories and contains around 615 calories in a 100 gm. It contains molybdenum, vitamin B-complex, manganese, copper, calcium, potassium, iron, selenium, vanadium, and zinc in abundance. Rich in dozens of phenolic acids, tannins—particularly ellagitannins—and flavonoids, walnut is also a good source of vitamin E. It also consists of:

- 14 per cent water
- 15 per cent protein
- 13 per cent carbohydrate
- 60 per cent fat

25
Figs

'To eat figs off the tree in the very early morning, when they have been barely touched by the sun, is one of the exquisite pleasures of the Mediterranean.'

—Elizabeth David

Fig, a member of the mulberry family, is a bulbous, luscious, and sweet fruit. When a fresh fig is cut in half, one can see the fleshy thread-bearing seeds. Fig is available in many varieties. Few of its varieties are not edible and were earlier considered as the food for goats. It is known in the culinary world for the chewiness of its flesh and the crunchiness of its seeds. Its significance is highly acknowledged for its horde of benefits for humankind.

Figs are packed with numerous phytochemicals and polyphenols. Phytochemicals—like flavonoids, gallic acid, epicatechins, rutin, and chlorogenic acid—and monosaccharide sugar are present in the fig's skin and seeds. Dark-coloured figs are rich in phytochemicals as compared to light-coloured figs. Even ripe and dried figs contain more polyphenols and sugar than unripe figs.

Below are some more qualities of figs:

- Figs are an excellent source of dietary fibre. They help maintain weight as they provide one with a sense of satiety.
- Potassium is plenty in figs. The intake of excess sodium by an individual results in the low absorption of potassium, leading to a deficiency. High sodium, low potassium intake leads to conditions like hypertension. Potassium is efficient in balancing blood pressure and hypertension as well. Its consumption decreases both systolic and diastolic pressure.

  Note: *Systolic blood pressure is the top number in the blood pressure scale, indicating the amount of pressure in arteries during contraction of heart muscles. Diastolic blood pressure is the bottom number, indicating blood pressure when heart muscle is between the beats. For illustration, if 120/80mm Hg is the blood pressure, 120 indicates systolic pressure and 80 indicates diastolic pressure.*
- The leaves of the fig tree are also known for their medicinal value. These leaves are edible and ficusin (the extract from fig leaves) display strong anti-diabetic properties. Its consumption ensures a balanced insulin in one's body. It also helps in normalising the level of blood fatty acids and vitamin E. Thus, fig leaves help in diabetic conditions as well.

  Note: *Insulin, a hormone produced by pancreas, allows the body to use sugar present in carbohydrates in the food being consumed. Insulin controls blood sugar levels as well and prevents it from being too high (hyperglycaemia) or from being too low (hypoglycaemia).*
- Figs are also beneficial for eyes and help maintain great vision, especially during old age.

- Figs are useful in easing numerous skin disorders like eczema, psoriasis, and vitiligo. In fact, applying the latex (milky fluid) of the fig tree aids in breaking down of warts—small and firm growth on the skin—automatically. Mashed raw figs are also used to prepare a rich face pack for a smooth and good skin.
- Nutrients like vitamin C, vitamin B, selenium, copper, magnesium, and zinc strengthen hair as well. Figs make the hair follicles strong and prevent hair loss.
- Vitamin K is found in abundance in figs, and it is a nutrient that aids in the clotting of blood.

  Note: *A person on blood-thinning medications should avoid figs.*
- Figs are packed with several polyphenolic-flavonoid antioxidants like tannins, chlorogenic acids, lutein, and carotenes. They are also packed with vitamins A and E. All these components combine to fight free radicals, shielding an individual from degenerative diseases like cancer, diabetes, and even several infections.
- Figs also act as an aphrodisiac. Moreover, they also help in improving one's reproductive health.
- Chlorogenic acid present in figs assists in lowering the blood sugar levels and controlling glucose levels, thus, preventing the chances of diabetes mellitus—a form of diabetes happening due to insulin deficiency, which results in the incapability to metabolise sugars and starch.

  Other sources of chlorogenic acids are: Apples, pears, tomatoes, sweet potatoes, carrots, coffee, and tea.

- The B-complex vitamins—niacin, pyridoxine, folates, and pantothenic acid—present in figs lead to the breakdown of carbohydrates, proteins, and fats. Thus, figs work towards the metabolism of all macronutrients.
- Being rich in dietary fibre content, fig provides volume to the stool, hence, facilitating a smooth and easy removal of body waste. Thus, adding figs to one's diet can lead to proper bowel movements and provide a sense of relief to those suffering from constipation.

Nutritive Highlights

Figs are an excellent source of dietary fibre and are low in calories; they contain 74 calories in a 100 gm. They are also a rich source of pantothenic acid, vitamin B6, vitamin A, vitamin K, folate, copper, calcium, manganese, and potassium. Figs also contain:

- 80 per cent water
- 0.76 per cent protein
- 0.3 per cent fat
- 20 per cent carbohydrate

26
Amla

'An Amla a day, keeps disease at bay.'

—AYUSH (Department of Health and Family Welfare, Government of India)

Amla, also known as Indian gooseberry, is a highly remarkable food ingredient indigenous to India and is acknowledged for its great medicinal values. It is a significant medicinal herb that is used as a tonic for its restorative qualities of lost energy and vitality. It is a fleshy pale-yellow fruit, which is sour in taste.

It is also revered for its blood-purifying qualities and its restorative mucous membrane—it is a tissue that secretes and that lines many body cavities and organs, too—characteristic. It is rich in vitamin C; in fact, the vitamin C found in 20 oranges can be obtained in just one amla.

Amla is composed of nutrients like tannins—Emblicanin A and B, punigluconin, geraniin, and ellagitannin—alkaloids, and phenols—gallic acid, ellagic acid, quercetin, and kaempferol. Amla is also the chief ingredient in many Ayurvedic preparations like Triphala, Brahma Rasayana, and Chyawanprash. Triphala is known for its multiple benefits and anti-ageing properties, whereas chyawanprash is known for its rejuvenating properties.

Amla is consumed in various forms, be it fresh, dried, liquid (juice), powder, or oil. Many people also make chutneys out of amla or pickle it, which is called *murrabba*. Its juice is also consumed all across the country by diluting it with water.

Some more qualities and benefits of amla are:

- Amla is packed with high contents of vitamin C and vitamin A, along with polyphenols, alkaloids, and flavonoids—such as quercetin and kaempferol. Due to the presence of such beneficial compounds, amla is a potent antibacterial and anti-inflammatory. Moreover, it is also a key player in boosting the immune system as it has the capacity to increase the number of white blood cells in the body.

  Other sources of quercetin are: Apple, onion, berries, red wine, green tea, broccoli, pepper, and grapes.

  Other sources of kaempferol are: Walnut, strawberry, raspberry, and blackberry.
- Amla contains chromium, which promotes a particular group of cells that releases insulin, thereby decreasing the blood sugar levels in those who suffer from diabetes. When the blood sugar level decreases after consuming amla, glucose is used by the cells, and this process improves one's metabolism by providing more energy, without tempering with the blood sugar levels.
- Rich in fibre, amla decreases the possibility of constipation. The fibre in amla adds volume to the stool and helps the food move easily through the bowels. Moreover, it also regulates the bowel movement. The soluble fibre loosens the bulky stools, reducing the chances of diarrhoea as well. Amla also promotes the release of gastric juices and digestive enzymes, making the overall digestion process smooth. It is effective

in keeping the digestive fire alive. Amla also has the extraordinary ability to retain water, which is crucial in preventing gastrointestinal disorders.

- Amla powder has the power to strengthen heart's muscles, which is the basic requirement for a better blood circulation. The chromium in amla has the ability to reduce the possibility of atherosclerosis in blood vessels. This decreases the risk of strokes and heart attacks. Amla is rich in iron, which rejuvenates the formation of red blood cells, improving blood circulation, oxygenating the cells, and regenerating tissues.
- As amla is rich in moisture, it is diuretic (causing increased passing of urine) in nature. Due to frequent and excessive passing of urine, excess, undesired, and harmful toxins are thrown out of the body. Thus, amla is beneficial for the health of kidney and preventing any urinary and uterine infections.
- Enriched with phytonutrients like quercetin, gallic acid, ellagic acid, it fights free radicals and acts as an antioxidant. It works towards detoxifying the entire body and is capable of removing harmful toxins and the after-effects of heavy medications as well.

  Other sources of gallic acid are: Red-coloured fruits, black radish, tea, and onions.

  Other sources of ellagic acid are: Walnut, strawberry, raspberry, and blackberry.
- Amla is a rich source of vitamin A and carotene, which makes it helpful in maintaining one's eyesight along with improving near-sightedness. It also aids in reducing the chances of macular degeneration and night blindness.

- Amla has the capability to restrict tumour growth, which can lead to several cancers. Amla is packed with various powerful polyphenols, flavonoids, and tannins. All these components have proved their cytotoxic (toxic to living cells) nature and their benefits in restricting cervical and ovarian cancer cells.
- The mineral and vitamin content in amla also aids in reducing menstrual cramps.
- Amla contains carotene, iron, and certain antioxidants, too. All these components make it highly desirable for strengthening the hair roots and avoiding premature greying. It is found that amla is also capable of adding shine to one's hair. It is quite effective in preventing hair loss and baldness.
- Amla ensures a better absorption of calcium in the body. Hence, it is remarkably useful in treating diarrhoea and dysentery.
- It acts as a relieving ingredient in the cases of burning sensation in the abdomen, which is known as hyperchlorhydria.
- When consumed with honey and butter before a meal, amla aids in improving and sparking one's appetite.
- It is also beneficial in conditions of cold, flu, and fever.

Nutritive Highlights

Amla is a rich source of vitamin C, nicotinic acid, and iron. It is a low-calorie fruit as it contains only 44 gm of calories in 100 gm of amla. It also consists of:

- 81.25 per cent water
- 0.5 per cent protein
- 14.1 per cent carbohydrate
- 0.1 per cent fat
- 0.7 per cent mineral content
- 3.4 per cent fibre
- 0.05 per cent calcium
- 0.02 per cent phosphorus

27
Pomegranate

'Observe a pomegranate—a tough shell protects the most delicious, delicate layered and beautiful jewel-like seeds that glow in the sunlight. But when the pomegranate falls to the ground, it will never be the same again, much like Alzheimer's and Dementia.'

—Paddick Van Zyl

Pomegranate, a member of Punicaceae family, is a blood-red fruit that has its seeds covered by arils—specialised outgrowth from a seed that partly or completely covers the seed. It is the most nutritive component of the fruit. Pomegranate is one of the healthiest fruits. It has unimaginable nutritive qualities that distinguish it from other fruits, which, in turn, makes it more desirable.

The fruit comprises of 80 per cent arils and 20 per cent seeds. The number of seeds in a fruit may range from 200 to 1,400. Aril is packed with 10 per cent sugars—fructose and glucose—and 1.5 per cent pectin, organic acid—ascorbic acid, malic acid, and citric acid—and bioactive compound like flavonoids and phenolics—majorly anthocyanins.

Some of the features of pomegranate are mentioned below:

- Tannins such as ellagitannin compounds like granatin B and punicalagin are present in huge amounts in pomegranates. It has been suggested that these tannins are efficient in decreasing the possibility of heart ailments by fighting the free radicals present in one's body. Pomegranate is one of the fruits that contain the maximum number of antioxidants and is exceptionally effective in removing the harmful effects of free radicals.

  Other sources of ellagitannin are: Walnut, almond, raspberry, and strawberry.

- Pomegranate provides around 17 per cent of the daily requirement of vitamin C in just a 100 gm. Thus, it is a rich source of vitamin C. Consuming pomegranate makes the body strong enough to fight with infectious diseases.

- Pomegranate seeds contain a high amount of potassium, an essential mineral required to normalise one's blood pressure, form muscles, and aid in the proper functioning of the nervous system. It also prevents atherosclerosis.

- The intake of pomegranate is effective in decreasing the level of systolic and diastolic blood concentration. Thus, it has a powerful impact in maintaining blood pressure level and improving the overall heart functions.

- The flavonoids in pomegranate are helpful in improving one's memory retention. It is found in lowering the risk of Alzheimer's and in fighting depression as well. Pomegranate juice contains estrone—a steroid, weak oestrogen, and a minor female sex hormone—which improves the mood in menopausal women.

- Pomegranate juice is effective in restricting the blood flow towards the tumour, leading to a decrease in its size and, finally, its destruction. The juice intake also has great impact in restricting the spread of cancerous cells in the human body, which reduces the chances of prostate and breast cancer. Thus, pomegranate is an effective anti-carcinogen.
- Pomegranate is a potent aphrodisiac, which has the ability to improve blood flow in an individual, thus, treating erectile dysfunction.
- Pomegranate, being rich in calcium and iron, is tremendously beneficial in increasing one's haemoglobin.
- Flavones are also present in pomegranates, which has powerful anti-inflammatory qualities. The enzymes—cyclooxygenase and lipoxygenase—lead to the degradation of extracellular joint matrix, and these enzymes are inhibited from function due to the antioxidants present in pomegranates. Thus, it provides relief from collagen-induced arthritis and osteoarthritis.
- The ellagic and gallic acids, present in pomegranates, are powerful natural antimicrobial agents. They have the capacity to fight against infections like diarrhoea and ulcers. It is also effective in providing relief in parasitic and bacterial infections, hence, improving respiratory conditions.
- The polyphenols present in pomegranates have the prebiotic potential to reduce the fat content of the body by reducing the cholesterol of a fat-rich diet and supporting the action in gut microbiota. It also helps in macrophage—it is a cell that destroys pathogens—

formation, prevents oxidation, and promotes better cardiovascular health.

- Punicic acid is one of the main constituents of pomegranate that helps in lowering cholesterol and triglycerides, in so doing, maintaining the blood pressure.
- The fibre content in pomegranate is helpful in improving one's bowel movements and boosting the digestive mechanism, thus, helping in providing relief to those who suffer from constipation.

Nutritive Highlights

Pomegranate contains 83 gm of calories in a 100 gm. It is also loaded with nutrients like calcium, iron, magnesium, potassium, phosphorus, vitamin C, vitamin K, and folate. It is made up of:

- 1.67 per cent protein
- 18.7 per cent carbohydrate
- 4 per cent dietary fibre
- 13.67 per cent sugar in a total of 100 gm
- 1.17 per cent fat

28
Jaggery

'Amidst these lanes of memories, your voice feels like can of jaggery with a weird taste, bitter yet sweet, without which life feels incomplete.'

—Anonymous

Jaggery, a natural and traditional sweetener, is a refined and processed form of sugar. It is made by unrefined sugar, which is obtained by reducing raw sugarcane juice. Jaggery is prepared from the sap of coconut or the sap of palm or sugarcane juice, but sugarcane juice is the widely used. Jaggery is much better in terms of health benefits to humankind as compared to sugar, which is nothing but a source of empty calories.

Described by its sugary taste, jaggery has gained popularity all across the globe. It has a yellowish-golden or brownish appearance and is loved for its sweet and wholesome flavour.

Some of the benefits and qualities of jaggery are:

- Jaggery is effective in stimulating the digestive enzymes, thus, resulting in better digestive system. It also promotes smooth bowel movements due to its high fibre content, keeping constipation at bay. It is diuretic in nature as well.

- Jaggery facilitates an easy removal of harmful toxins from the liver. In fact, jaggery is a natural body cleanser and is found to reduce the task performed by the liver, hence, increasing its efficiency.
- Consuming jaggery generates heat in the body. That is why, it is consumed mostly during winters. It also known to combat the symptoms of cold, cough, and flu.
- Some menstruating women experience premenstrual syndrome (PMS). Jaggery is known to release endorphins, which relaxes the body and provides relief from cramps as well.
- Jaggery has the power to purify blood, freeing one from several ailments and any disorders. In order to benefit from this, jaggery must be consumed in small quantities on a daily basis.
- Jaggery also acts as a natural cleansing agent by removing undesired and unwanted particles from the body. It has the efficiency to clean both the respiratory and digestive tract. Thus, apart from aiding in smooth digestion, it also keeps respiratory issues like asthma, bronchitis, etc., at bay.
- Jaggery is loaded with iron and folate (vitamin B9), which maintains one's haemoglobin as it keeps the level of red blood cells in check. In so doing, jaggery prevents the chances of anaemia.
- The calcium present in jaggery works wonders to improve issues associated with bones. It is found to keep certain bone ailments like arthritis and joint pain at bay.
- Potassium is also found in abundance in jaggery. This mineral is responsible for balancing electrolytes along

with building muscles and stimulating metabolism. Potassium actually works in decreasing the body's water retention. Thus, it works towards effective weight loss and maintaining weight, too.

- It also maintains proper acid levels in the body due to the presence of potassium and sodium. Thus, it aids in maintaining one's blood pressure.
- Jaggery is packed with heavy carbohydrate content and when consumed, it easily gets absorbed in the blood stream, providing instant energy. Thus, it helps in preventing fatigue in an individual.
- Jaggery is also rich in selenium and zinc, which perform the functions of antioxidants. It aids in fighting harmful free radicals. It improves the body's resistance against infections as well.
- Jaggery is also known for its anti-allergic properties.
- When consumed with amla powder, jaggery has the capability to improve sperm quality and boost its production, too.

Note: *Due to high calorie content—of around 380 calories in a 100 gm—if jaggery is consumed in large quantities, it can lead to obesity. An excess intake of jaggery also leads to an increase in blood sugar levels. If not consumed with proper precautions, jaggery may cause parasitic infections. Freshly prepared jaggery is hard to digest and may result in diarrhoea. Fresh jaggery can also lead to constipation in a few individuals. If consumed excessively during summers, it may lead to nosebleeds due to its warm temperament. It may also increase inflammation as it interferes with the absorption of Omega-3 fatty acids. Lastly, jaggery should not be consumed with fish as the human body doesn't like this combination.*

Nutritive Highlights

Jaggery is a rich food in terms of calories; it has around 380 calories in a 100 gm. It is an excellent source of vitamin B6, pantothenic acid, calcium, iron, magnesium, potassium, selenium, and manganese. It also contains folate (vitamin B9), niacin (vitamin B3), betaine (modified amino acids), and choline (essential nutrient neither vitamin nor mineral) in small amounts. It consists of:

- 85–95 per cent carbohydrate—like sucrose, fructose, and glucose
- Less than 1 per cent protein
- Less than 1 per cent fat
- 4 per cent moisture

29
Carrots

'Who cares if a carrot has a slight bend? They're all the same when they end up on the plate.'
—Tristram Stuart

Carrot is a root vegetable that is cherished the most amongst all other root vegetables. Available in various colours such as yellow, orange, red, white, and purple, its taproot is extremely valued for its use in salads and other culinary preparations. Carrot is flat at top end and tapered at the lower end. Few carrots are cylindrical in shape with a rounded end. It can be consumed raw as well as cooked. It is incorporated in numerous salads, soups, and various delicacies.

It has a woody element on top and many choose to remove it before consuming as it doesn't taste as good. Appreciated for its crunchy texture and sweet taste, carrot has multiple nutritional benefits, which makes it another superfood.

The colour of carrot is distinguished by distinct phytonutrients like bright orange carrot contains alpha-carotene and beta-carotene, purple carrot is enriched with anthocyanin, yellow carrot contains lutein, and red contains lycopene in abundance.

Carrots contain ample quantities of antioxidants and phytonutrients like carotenoids—majorly alpha-carotene and lutein; hydroxycinnamic acids—caffeic, coumaric, and ferulic; anthocyanins—cyanidins and malvidins, which is present in red and purple carrots; and polyacetylenes—falcarinol and falcarindiol.

Note: *Hydroxycinnamic acid exhibits potent antioxidant properties, anti-collagenase, anti-inflammatory, antimicrobial protection from ultraviolet rays and has anti-ageing qualities as well.*

Some more features and benefits of carrots are mentioned below:

- Carrot is packed with ample vitamin A. Its deficiency leads to progressive eye disorders like xerophthalmia, a condition wherein the eye fails to produce tears. Carrots are also rich in antioxidants—lutein and zeaxanthin—and both these components helps in delaying and preventing macular degeneration.
- Carotenes, natural antioxidants, play a key role in the human body as they help in the formation of vitamin A in the liver converting themselves. It fights free radicals, maintains eye health, improves reproduction, and boosts sperm production.
- An antioxidant (of polyacetylene group) called falcarinol is also present in carrots. It is believed that it may help in combating cancers as it destroys the pre-cancerous cells in tumours. Carotenoid is also regarded as a potent anti-carcinogen as it reduces the risk of prostate, lung, and colon cancers.
- Carrot is full of potassium and is rich in fibre as well. Both the nutrients aid in maintaining blood pressure. Potassium also helps in relaxing blood vessels, thereby decreasing the possibility of high blood pressure, which,

in turn, reduces the chances of cardiovascular issues. Fibre consumption also lowers the bad cholesterol in the bloodstream.

- Carrot contains sufficient amount of vitamin C and is responsible for collagen production. Collagen is a chief element in connective tissues, which is necessary for healing wounds. Vitamin C also improves the immune system, fighting and preventing various diseases and infections.
- Carrot also contains dietary fibres which benefits the digestive system greatly. Fibre also helps increase the volume of the stool and let it pass conveniently through the digestive tract, avoiding constipation.
- Chewing carrots help neutralise the traces of citric and malic acids in the mouth, thus, improving one's oral health.

Note:

- ➢ *White blush is a phenomenon that occurs in carrots when they are peeled and a white coat on its peeled flesh is formed. Peeling the outermost layer of carrots makes it difficult for them to maintain their moisture level. This dehydration forms the above-mentioned white blush. Soaking pealed carrots in water is advised.*
- ➢ *Carrots experience a huge loss of micronutrients like potassium, zinc, iron, calcium, magnesium, and phosphorus if they are cooked for too long. In order to receive optimum benefits of their mineral content, it is advised to cook carrots for a short duration and that, too, by steaming.*
- ➢ *Carotenoderma is a condition in which, due to excessive consumption of carotene-rich foods, one's skin turns*

yellowish-orange in colour. The excessive amount of carotene in the blood is called carotenemia. This condition disappears when the consumption of carotene-rich foods is stopped or reduced.

Nutritive Highlights

Carrots contain calcium, magnesium, potassium, phosphorus, and sodium in abundance. They are also composed of copper, zinc, manganese, selenium, and various other vitamins in small amounts. Carrots are also packed with antioxidants and extremely beneficial phytonutrients. They provide around 41 calories in a 100 gm. Carrots also consist of:

- 89 per cent water
- Less than 1 per cent protein
- Less than 1 per cent fat
- 9.5 per cent carbohydrate (out of which 30 per cent is dietary fibre and rest is sugar)

30

Coconut

'The two basic items to sustain life are sunshine and coconut milk.'

—Dustin Hoffman

Coconut is a seed or fruit of the palm tree family. Even though its name suggests that it is a nut, it is, in fact, a drupe fruit, aka stone fruit. The large oval and brown seeds of the tropical palm tree consist of a hard shell that is lined with edible white flesh and contains a clear liquid inside it. Surrounded by fibre, it is acknowledged for its versatility as all of its components—flesh, water, milk, and oil—are used and cherished tremendously.

Coconut water is an elixir, which contains around 94 per cent water and trace amount of all other nutrients, whereas coconut milk contains around 50 per cent water with fat and protein as its other components. Coconut water is also considered the best thirst quencher and is quite refreshing and nutritious. Coconut also has religious significance attached to it.

Below are some more characteristics and benefits of coconut:

- Coconut water is extremely refreshing and nutritious. It is effective in beating the tropical summer heat, and its electrolyte composition (potassium) makes it an ideal drink for hydrating the body in conditions like dehydration, diarrhoea, vomiting, or excessive sweating. Along with hydrating the body, it also provides comfort to the stomach and is used to help in ailments like indigestion and gastroenteritis.
- Cytokinin—a class of phytohormones—is the chief component of coconut water. It exhibits strong anti-ageing properties along with being an antioxidant. It also shows strong anti-cancer characteristics and has anti-platelet properties as well.
- Coconut water is fat-free and helps in decreasing bad cholesterol level while boosting the good cholesterol. It also has an impressive effect on lipid metabolism to combat cholesterol and triglycerides levels. Coconut water also reduces the chances of plaque formation in the arteries, which reduces the possibility of heart attacks and strokes.
- Coconut water is low in calories and is packed with various bioactive enzymes that expedite proper digestion and bolster lipid metabolism as well. The sodium, when in excess, results in water retention in the body, leading to an increase in weight. But as coconut water is packed with potassium, its consumption balances the sodium present in the body. The electrolytes present in the water are also helpful in relieving muscle cramps.
- Migraine—a throbbing headache affecting one side of the head often accompanied by nausea and perturbed vision—usually occurs due to extreme dehydration and low level of magnesium. Coconut water not only

hydrated the body but supplies it with magnesium as well, which provides relief with migraines.

- Coconut water has ample water-soluble B-complex vitamins like vitamin B1, vitamin B2, vitamin B3, vitamin B5, vitamin B6, vitamin B7, vitamin B9. All these vitamins are crucial for acting as coenzymes for enzymatic reactions to carry out cellular functions. They are also needed for the smooth functioning of the human body. Folates are used to cure anaemia in pregnant women. In fact, vitamin B6 is a great anti-inflammatory.
- Coconut water contains vitamin C, potassium, and magnesium, and these nutrients help in controlling high blood pressure. Potassium has the ability to lower the blood pressure by balancing the side effects of sodium.
- Excessive consumption of alcohol results in dehydration, which is why one feels hungover the next morning. As coconut water is rich in water content, it hydrates the body and fights free radicals as well.
- Coconut is rich in dietary fibre, which slows down the release of glucose in the body and transports it to the cell where it gets converted into energy. It helps in decreasing stress on enzymatic system and pancreas, decreasing the possibility of diabetes. Coconut also boosts the secretion of insulin. Coconut fibre improves the digestion process, making it beneficial in controlling diabetes and stimulating the digestive system.
- As coconut is high in fat and low in carbohydrates, it treats several disorders, especially epilepsy, in children.
- Monolaurin and lauric acid, a saturated fatty acid present in coconut, is able to fight and kill bacteria, virus, and fungus. This keeps infections at bay.

- Other sources of lauric acid are: Extra virgin olive oil, sesame oil, corn oil, and peanut butter.
- Coconut is also capable of burning fat, which results in weight loss. It is also capable of reducing hunger pangs as it metabolises the fatty acids in the body and releases ketone—an organic compound—which reduces appetite. It has been studied that people who consume coconut flesh do not eat as often and show no symptoms of hypoglycaemia—unusually low blood sugar leading to a poor diet. It also is beneficial for those who have thyroid. Moreover, coconut provides energy as well.
- Coconut is a great antiviral, antifungal, antibacterial, and antiparasitic. Thus, it treats ailments like throat infections, urinary tract infection, and other disorders that occur due to microbes.

Nutritive Highlights

Coconut provides a high number of calories; around 355 calories in just 100 gm of coconut flesh. It is an excellent source of high saturated fatty acids like lauric acid, few bioactive compounds, folates, niacin, pyridoxine, manganese, selenium, copper, potassium, phosphorus, iron, and zinc.
It also contains:

- 5 per cent protein
- 15 per cent carbohydrate
- 70 per cent dietary fibre
- 50 per cent sugar
- 34 per cent fat

31

Sprouts

'You need a green thumb in order to grow a flowering vegetable or a fruit tree or garden. The sprouts are however very simple, yet extremely nutritious'

—Doug Evans, *The Sprout Book*

Sprouts are the edible germinated seeds that have turned into young plants. They are one of the most nutritious foods on this planet. The germination process is initiated by soaking the seeds in water for several hours. Then, the soaked seeds are removed from water and exposed to appropriate temperature and moisture. This stage takes 2 to 6 days, depending upon the seeds and the environment they are exposed to. In a few days, the seeds shoot up in the form of sprouts that are about 2–5 cm long.

There are several sprouted seeds like chickpeas, lentils, soybean, kidney beans, peas, and mung beans, and their benefits can be derived if consumed on a regular basis.

Some of the benefits of sprouts are mentioned below:

- Chickpea sprouts are quite easy to make and are high in protein and several other nutrients as well. They consist of isoflavones—a class of phytoestrogen, a plant-based compound—which are extremely beneficial for women going through menopause. They are also beneficial to those suffering from osteoporosis and high cholesterol. Chickpeas are a rich source of protein, carbohydrates, vitamin C, and iron; they provide 340 calories in a 100 gm.

- Lentil sprouts provide 106 calories in a 100 gm. The sprouting in lentil increases the phenolic content by 122 per cent! Phenolic compounds are antioxidants that can combat cancer, inflammation, and various allergies. The sprouted lentils decrease bad cholesterol, thereby fighting heart diseases, obesity, and diabetes.
- Soybean sprouts comprises 122 calories in a 100 gm. Soyabean is also low in protein and carbohydrate content but contains vitamin C, folate, and iron as well. Soybean contains phytic acid—an antinutrient—which hampers the absorption of iron in the body. But sprouted soybean has around 55 per cent less phytic acid. The consumption of soybean sprouts increases the level of iron in the body as it doesn't interfere with its absorption as compared to non-sprouted soybeans. Thus, it treats anaemia and increases the level of ferritin—protein that is produced to store iron in the tissues—as well.
- Kidney bean sprouts are a rich source of protein. They provide 29 calories in a 100 gm, making them low in calories. They are also rich in vitamin C, folate, and iron. Kidney bean sprouts contain melatonin—a hormone released from the endocrine glands of brain and it restricts melanin formation by regulation of reproduction cycle—which is useful in fighting diabetes and lowers the risk of heart diseases.

- Both green and yellow peas can be sprouted. Extremely nutritious, they offer 125 calories in a 100 gm. Pea sprouts are rich in vitamin C, folate, and iron. The sprouted peas contain double the amount of folate as compared to raw peas. The folic acid in these sprouts is used to treat neural tube defects—defect associated with nervous system wherein the bones surrounding the child's spine or skull in the womb doesn't develop properly and leads to several complications.
- Mung beans are enormously low in calories, delivering just 30 calories in a 100 gm. They are low in protein and carbohydrates and contain vitamin C, folate, and iron as well. The process of sprouting mung beans multiplies the amount of flavonoid by 7 times and vitamin C by 24 times. It is an anti-carcinogen in nature.
- In the arena of nutrition, only seeds or beans are preferred for sprouting and consumption. Sprouted foods are, undoubtedly, the economical way to make food more nutritious as they contain a high concentration of vitamin E, bioflavonoids—combination of multivitamins with, copper, manganese, and zinc—antioxidants, phytochemicals, potassium, iron, chemoprotectants—compounds protecting from the after-effects of chemicals used in chemo—and protein.
- Sprouts should not be cooked as exposure to heat makes them lose their nutritive value. Sprouts can be consumed with tomatoes, broccoli, onion, radish, and cucumber to enhance their taste. Steamed sprouts, too, lose some of their nutrient components but are easily digestible.

- Sprouts increase the number of enzymes in one's food—100 times more as compared to uncooked fruits and vegetables. The amount of lysine (amino acid) and fibre content, too, increases manifold. Certain vitamins are found to increase by around 20 times when sprouted—vitamin B1 by 280 per cent, vitamin B2 by 500 per cent, and niacin by 250 per cent—and the amount of essential fatty acids also increases.
- Sprouts are the powerhouse of nutrients and comprises decent amount of certain organic compounds and nutrients like protein, dietary fibre and vitamins like vitamin K, folate, pantothenic acid, niacin, vitamin C, vitamin A, riboflavin, and thiamine. They also include minerals like calcium, magnesium, iron and zinc.
- Sprouts are known to alkalise our body, counteracting the excess acidity.
- Sprouts are loaded with vitamin C, which works as an antioxidant and helps in bolstering the immune system. It stimulates the white blood cells, which combats infections effectively.
- Sprouts have a high number of enzymes, due to which they are capable of boosting numerous metabolic processes and chemical reactions inside the body, aiding digestion. Moreover, its rich fibre content adds volume to the stool and helps in the smooth functioning of the digestive system. Dietary fibre also promotes gastric juices, which, in combination with the already-existing enzymes, stimulates digestion.
- Sprouts are also rich in protein, and protein plays a key role in bone and muscle development, organ repair, and the maintenance of cells. Sprouts are a blessing for vegetarians due to their protein content.

- Sprouts are also packed with iron, which helps in fighting fatigue, lack of concentration, stomach ailments, and nausea. It also helps in maintaining the red blood cells, which are necessary for a smooth blood circulation in our body, thereby supplying sufficient oxygen to all the organs. The proper blood flow also helps treat erectile dysfunction.
- A source of Omega-3 fatty acids—alpha-linolenic acid (ALA) in particular—sprouts have the ability to decrease triglycerides in the blood. This essential fatty acid works as a potent anti-inflammatory agent, decreasing the stress on one's cardiovascular system. It is also rich in potassium, which aids in lowering one's blood pressure and releasing tension in the arteries and blood vessels. Thus, avoiding the possibility of atherosclerosis, heart attacks, and strokes.
- Vitamin B is also present in plenitude in sprouts and this helps in hydrating the skin. It is effective in reducing acne and premature wrinkles.

Nutritive Highlights

The nutritive values of sprouts depend on the kind of sprouts one is consuming. What is common in all the varieties of sprouts is that they are a powerhouse of nutrients and rich in antioxidants.

They are rich in iron, folate, vitamin C, vitamin A, and protein.

32
Guava

'A guava tree in bloom, for instance, lost in the pages of a good novel, can bring delight with its fictional perfume to any number of real rooms.'
—José Edvardo Agualusa

Guava is one of the most loved fruits that is incorporated in salads, desserts, smoothies, and even juices due to its multifaceted characteristic of being crunchy and subtle in taste. It has a light green, yellow or maroon colour when it ripens, and has a white or maroon flesh with small, hard seeds in its soft, delicious pulp.

A round and pear-shaped tropical fruit, guava has charmed everyone with its splendid taste and treasure trove of health benefits. Recognised for its nature to balance hormones impeccably, it has a low Glycaemic Index and is found to not increase the level of sugar in the bloodstream.

Guava is packed with numerous antioxidants and phytochemicals along with essentials oils, polysaccharides, minerals, vitamins, enzymes, steroids, glycosides, tannins, flavonoids, carotenoids, and saponins. It contains a large amount of pectin.

It also has the following features:

- Guava is packed with compounds like gallic acid, galangin (polyphenol—flavonoid), kaempferol, cyanidin 3-glucoside in its peel, pulp, and seeds. Surprisingly, the pulp of guava contains less amount of these compounds as compared to its peel and skin. These compounds make guava a potent anti-carcinogen in nature, with tremendous properties of antioxidants to fight the harmful free radicals.

  Other sources of gallic acid are: Grapes, plum, strawberry, mango, cashew nut, walnut, tea, and wine.

  Other sources of cyanidin 3-glucoside compounds are: Black soybean, and blueberries.

  Other sources of kaempferol are: Grapes, apples, broccoli, onion, cucumber, lettuce, peaches, spinach, tomatoes, and potatoes.

- Compounds like quercetin, ferulic acid, ascorbic acid, caffeic acid, gallic acid, and protocatechuic acid are all outstanding antioxidants present in guava, which makes it a fruit of great worth and unimaginable medicinal capabilities. It is capable of providing relief against diseases like cancer, brain disorders, heart diseases, arthritis, and atherosclerosis.

  Other sources of ferulic acid are: Rice, wheat, pineapples, vegetables, beans, coffee seeds, peanuts, and nuts.

  Other sources of caffeic acid are: Coffee, wine, apples, pears, and berries.

  Other sources of protocatechuic acid are: Brown rice grain, olive oil, plum, star anise, and white grapes.

- The fibre content in guava gives a feeling of fullness to an individual and it makes sure that there are no unusual ups and downs in one's glucose levels.

The fibre in guava also decreases the possibility of haemorrhoids.

- Vitamin A in guava helps boost one's eye health. It cuts down the possibility of cataract and macular degeneration.
- Guava contains vitamin C along with ample lycopene. Both these components are effective in increasing the radiance of the skin by making it smooth and youthful. Being rich in moisture, it helps in hydrating the skin as well.

  Other sources of lycopene are: Tomatoes, watermelon, papaya, and grapefruit.
- Guava has electrolyte potassium in it, which counters the side effects of sodium in our body. This function of potassium allows controlling the blood pressure by lowering it. Potassium is extremely efficient in maintaining water balance and performing electrolytic functions in the body.
- Guava is rich in compounds like terpenes and p-selinene, and it has been studied that such compounds are capable of relaxing an individual.

  Other sources of terpenes are: Broccoli, beer, citrus fruits, apples, and mangoes.
- Manganese is also present in a good amount in guava. This micronutrient, though required in small amount by the human body, provides a crucial function by promoting other food nutrients to be effectively absorbed in the body.
- The leaves of the guava tree also help in fighting microbial and bacterial infections. Its leaves contain terpinene and pinene, which make them a great

antimicrobial. Moreover, it also acts as an antiviral; hence it functions effectively against influenza viruses and certain microbes and bacteria, too. In fact, the leaves of the guava tree leaves are used in various medicines to combat cough, diarrhoea, mouth ulcers, and swollen gums.

- Since guava is rich in antioxidants, it stimulates and boosts immunity in an individual. Due to this property, it fights infections. It also protects the cells from being damaged.
- Guava is a fruit that can be consumed without a second thought by those who have diabetes. It is high in dietary fibre, which plays a key role in decreasing the blood glucose levels.

Nutritive Highlights

Guava is an excellent source of vitamin C, vitamin K, vitamin A, niacin, folates, calcium, iron, magnesium, potassium, and phosphorous. It contains 68 calories in a 100 gm. It also consists of:

- 80 per cent water
- 2.55 per cent protein
- Less than 1 per cent fat
- 14.32 per cent carbohydrate
  - 8.92 per cent sugar
  - 5.4 per cent fibre in a 100 gm

33
Wheatgrass

'Wheatgrass juice is the nectar of rejuvenation, the plasma of youth, the blood of life.'
—Viktoras Kulvinskas

Wheatgrass is a food made from the green, young grass of the wheat plant, Triticum aestivum. It is harvested in a period of 5 to 7 days and is immature as compared to the actual wheat crop. It is light green in colour and is an exceptional source of many vitamins and minerals. It can be consumed in the form of juice or powder. It can be consumed as a super tonic on a daily basis in order to avoid and treat many illnesses. Though, its benefits are still being researched.

Wheatgrass can be easily grown indoors. Its leaves are considered consumable and highly nutritious when they spilt, also known as the 'jointing stage'. It is cut from the top to allow further growth and, then, it harvested.

It is also known as 'Green Blood' as it comprises 70 per cent chlorophyll, due to which it attains its green colour. It contains ample vitamins, minerals, amino acids, and certain important enzymes such as superoxide dismutase and cytochrome oxidase. It is also loaded with bioflavonoids. One surprising fact is that out of the 102 elements found in the soil, 98 elements, alone, are present in wheatgrass!

Some of the benefits of wheatgrass are:

- Chlorophyll is the key component of wheatgrass. The molecules of chlorophyll are quite similar to hemin, which combines with protein to form haemoglobin. The central atom of chlorophyll is magnesium, whereas haemoglobin has iron. All the benefits of this green product revolve around this chief component. Chlorophyll is the most effective when it is obtained from a living plant. It functions as a blood builder and improves the platelet count as well.
- Wheatgrass is undoubtedly a rich source of chlorophyll, laetrile, and superoxide dismutase—an enzyme. All these compounds are blessed with the ability to convert free radicals into hydrogen peroxide and oxygen. Hydrogen peroxide and oxygen molecules have immense power to kill cancer cells and restrict their growth. Wheatgrass also contains abscisic acid, a plant hormone, which is more efficient in neutralising chorionic gonadotropin, a hormone, which produces cancer cells. Wheatgrass juice is highly alkaline in nature and cancer cells find themselves uncomfortable in an alkaline medium. The antioxidant properties of wheatgrass restrict the proliferation of cancer cells and prevent damage to deoxyribonucleic acid (DNA) as well. Wheatgrass has been an effective remedy in treating and prohibiting the risk of liver, colon, and stomach cancers. Wheatgrass sprouts also possess the quality to restrict the metabolic activities of carcinogens, thereby decreasing their cancer-causing power by around 99 per cent.
- Choline is a component present in wheatgrass and helps in preventing fat accumulation around the liver.

Choline also stimulates the removal of cholesterol and esters from the liver, promoting its smooth functioning.

- Chlorophyll comprises enzymes and superoxide dismutase, and both these compounds help in reversing the effects of ageing. Chlorophyll contains more light energy than any other food ingredient as it is the first product of light. Thus, it is more energetic in nature.
- Wheatgrass also restricts the growth of harmful bacteria. It is antibacterial in nature and acts as a natural healer. In fact, liquid chlorophyll refines and rejuvenates the tissues.
- Chlorophyll detoxifies our system by removing toxins, purifying the liver, and improving blood sugar issues as well.
- Chlorophyll has the power to maintain the smooth functioning of the heart, vascular system, intestines, lungs, and uterus.
- Chlorophyll also helps in removing the scarring on lungs due to breathing acid gases. The ill effects of carbon monoxide are reduced as it boosts haemoglobin production in the body.
- Wheatgrass juice is good for treating sore throat and pyorrhoea—a condition where inflammation occurs in the teeth sockets, generating pus. It also avoids tooth decay and aches of any sort.
- Chlorophyll in wheatgrass juice has bacteriostatic (restricting bacteria) properties, healing the wound and increasing haemoglobin. It is used in treating skin lesions, burns, and ulcers by promoting granulation tissue—new blood vessel tissues in granular form on an ulcer or on the surface of the wound.

Nutritive Highlights

Wheatgrass juice is packed with a rich nutrient content. It is an excellent source of beta-carotene, vitamin C, vitamin E, vitamin B12, calcium, phosphorus, iron, and magnesium. Wheatgrass is also a rich source of crucial components like ferulic acid, sinapic acid, glutamic acid, histidine, threonine, arginine, citrulline, and leucine. It delivers 99 calories in 100 ml juice, which has:

- 1.82 per cent protein
- 0.49 per cent fat
- 25.31 per cent carbohydrate
    - more than 50 per cent fibre

34
CURRY LEAVES

'Most of us are like curry leaves, just added and used up for flavouring. Once we become nothing, thrown away like a fallen leaf, unwanted and unattended.'

—Sreepriya Menon

In the culinary world, curry leaves are considered the most fragrant leaves of all. They have the capability of adding a new dimension to a dish. Curry leaves are green in colour, highly aromatic, and smooth. Its undersides are paler in appearance. These aromatic leaves are bitter and pungent in taste.

The most crucial components of curry leaves are carbazole alkaloids, which include mahanimbine, murrayanol, bismahanine, and isomahanine. These compounds give the curry leaves their fragrance along with being antimicrobial, insecticidal, and mosquitocidal. The leaves are either grounded or are consumed whole or in the form of juice. Volatile oils are extracted out of curry leaves, which are then used for various purposes. It is used to temper various savoury preparations and is incorporated in numerous Indian delicacies. Moreover, due to their medicinal properties, curry leaves are highly revered in the field of Ayurveda.

Below are some of its features and benefits:

- Curry leaves are associated with hypoglycaemia. They are beneficial for those who suffer from a high blood sugar. Consuming curry leaves decreases the blood sugar by producing insulin from the pancreatic cells. They also aid in reducing the breakdown of starch into glucose, lowering glucose levels in the blood.
- Curry leaves contain ample volatile essential oils like α-pinene, sabinene, β-pinene, α-terpinene, etc., which acts as an anti-inflammatory, antibacterial, antidysenteric, and carminative. Due to such medicinal benefits, they are great in maintaining one's hair, skin, and oral health.
- High concentration of iron makes curry leaves highly beneficial in increasing the haemoglobin and RBC count. So, consuming curry leaves can help in reducing or preventing anaemia and fatigue. They also function as natural blood purifiers, decreasing the possibility of infections.
- Curry leaves are capable of stimulating digestive enzymes, leading to a better digestive system. They also support the bowel movement; hence, they are helpful in curing diarrhoea, dysentery, and constipation.
- Curry leaves are rich in fibre, which also serves well in several gastrointestinal ailments. Their carminative, antiemetic, and antidysenteric features decrease the possibility of conditions like piles, nausea, and bloating. It is also effective in improving one's appetite.
- The carbazole alkaloids present in curry leaves are capable of decreasing the LDL cholesterol in the bloodstream. Thus, it prevents one from gaining excess

weight. Moreover, it helps in removing toxins from the body.

- The volatile oil in curry leaves like linalool is effective in lowering the stress and anxiety levels, and in some cases depression as well. The fragrance of the oil is known to soothe and calm one's mind, making them feel relaxed.
- Curry leaves have been used in treating various dental problems due to their antibacterial and antimicrobial nature. They aid in maintaining proper oral health, and the volatile oil strengthens the gums and teeth, along with removing foul odour from the mouth.
- Due to the large amount of calcium present in it, curry leaves are effective in preventing disease like osteoporosis and osteomalacia—softening of the bones due to calcium deficiency. Thus, curry leaves play a key role in improving one's bone health.
- The phenols and carbazole alkaloids in the curry leaves are anti-carcinogen in nature. They help in preventing prostate and colorectal cancers. They also provide relief to those going through chemotherapy and radiotherapy.
- Curry leaves are also significant players in treating morning sickness. The digestive secretion increases and provides relief in such a case.
- Carbazole alkaloid is a great compound in healing various cuts and bruises. It is helpful in treating skin infections, burns, and wounds.
- Vitamin A, found in abundance in curry leaves, plays a huge role in improving one's eyesight. It also prevents the chances of cataract.

- Curry leaves are also rich in vitamin A and β-carotene. Both these nutrients play a significant role in treating eye ailments such as drying of the cornea. Thus, it lowers the risk of xeropthalmia and night blindness.
- It is believed that curry leaves are also useful in improving an individual's retention and brain power. They also treat brain disease like Alzheimer's.
- The presence of tannins and carbazole alkaloids is excellent in treating hepatoprotective properties. Thus, curry leaves have been used in protecting the liver from several diseases like hepatitis and cirrhosis. The antioxidants present in them, like kaempferol—a type of flavonoid, are found to fight free radicals, protecting the liver from toxins.

  Other sources of kaempferol are: Walnut, strawberry, raspberry, blackberry, and amla.

Nutritive Highlights

Curry leaves are enriched with compounds like alkaloids, flavonoids, and sterols. Moreover, they comprise multiple vitamins like nicotinic acid, vitamin A, vitamin C, vitamin B, and vitamin E, and minerals like magnesium, copper, iron, phosphorus, and calcium. It has no fat content. Curry leaves also consist of:

- 61–62 per cent moisture
- 2–12 per cent protein
- 14.6–19 per cent sugar
- 9.7–13 per cent ash content
- 1–1.8 per cent acid insoluble ash

35

Dates

'He who eats seven dates every morning, will not be affected by poison or magic on the day he eats them.'

—Prophet Muhammad

Dates are a fruit of the date palm tree, grown in several tropical regions. They are used quite a bit in the Middle East as they are found in abundance there. The date fruits are cylindrical in shaped, with 1–3 inches long. They are bright red to dark purple in colour. Dates are firm and crunchy in the initial stage of ripeness, and are sweeter and less firm during the later stage of ripeness. They are preferred when they are soft and sweet.

Marked by their sweet taste, dates are rich in carbohydrates. They are highly nutritional and have multiple benefits. As dates can be easily dried and preserved, they have a longer shelf life. Dates are an inexpensive source of nutrients. The best part about them is that this quality makes them exceptional than any other sweet foods or fruits.

Dates have numerous advantages over other sweet fruits:

- Fructose is the disaccharide, which imparts dates their sweet taste. The best part is that fructose does not increase the blood sugar levels as glucose does. Hence, the consumption of dates is an excellent way to indulge in sweets without worrying about any side effects.

- Dietary fibre is beneficial for one's health as it leads towards great cardiovascular health along with maintaining a proper balance of blood sugar and the digestive system as well. They also help in treating ailments like haemorrhoids. It is advised that men must consume 35 to 40 gm and women around 25 gm of dates every day.

  Other sources of dietary fibre are: Wholegrain wheat; barley; rye; fruits like berries, oranges, and melon; vegetables like broccoli, spinach, carrots, peas, beans, potatoes; nuts, and seeds.

- Dates also provide an abundance of trace minerals like selenium, which has many advantages. Selenium is responsible for becoming the part of the amino acids and forming the proteins required for enzymatic reactions. If there is a deficiency of selenium in any individual, it may put the individual under extreme physiological stress, leading to tissue damage. It has been proven that selenium intake decreases the possibility of cancer, especially bladder and prostate cancers. Its intake also leads to better cardiovascular health and stronger immune system as well.

  Other sources of selenium are: Rice, corn, wheat and other whole grains, seafood, offal, lean red meat, chicken, nuts, eggs, cheese, and legumes, and vegetables grown in selenium-rich soil.

- Dates are rich in antioxidants. Tannins, a type of polyphenolic antioxidant, are present in abundance in dates. It has been found that tannins reduce inflammation along with boosting the immune system. Dates are a great source of vitamin A and K. Both the vitamins have great antioxidant properties.

Other sources of tannins are: Thyme, oregano, cloves, cocoa powder, dark chocolate, berries, beans, and nuts.

- Potassium is another mineral that is required in small amounts by the body. It stimulates physiological processes and acts as an electrolyte, too. It also decreases the possibility of stroke, osteoporosis, high blood pressure, and kidney stones. Dates have plenty potassium content, and just a couple of dates can provide upto 10 per cent of potassium.

  Other sources of potassium are: Cucumber, spinach, broccoli, mushroom, peas, bananas, oranges, raisin, and prunes.

- Minerals like selenium, manganese, copper, and magnesium in dates are essential for one's bone health. Dates supply these minerals, hence, providing relief from bone-related ailments.
- Dates also have magnesium in them, which is blessed with anti-inflammatory properties. Because of these anti-inflammatory properties, dates are beneficial in conditions like Alzheimer's, arthritis, and even several issues related to the heart.
- The combination of potassium and magnesium in dates makes it more valuable for cardiovascular health as both these minerals have the power to decrease blood pressure and facilitate the smooth functioning of the heart. As per one study, conducted by The American Journal of Clinical Nutrition, researchers found that small amounts of magnesium—just 100 milligrams—on a daily basis decreases one's possibility of strokes.

- Consuming dates during pregnancy, especially four months prior to delivery, can improve labour parameters, along with delivery outcomes. This was found in the research conducted by Jordan University of Science and Technology.
- Dates also act as an effective aphrodisiac and improve the sexual stamina of an individual. If consumed with a glass of warm milk, it has the ability to prevent sterility and several sexual disorders.
- Due to their versatility and multiple benefits, dates are effective in preventing stomach, ovarian, pancreatic, renal, colorectal, and liver cancer. Thus, eating dates on a regular basis prevents various cancers in the abdomen.
- Vitamins like vitamin B6 and minerals like potassium in dates are responsible for improving the nervous system along with more responsive and alert brain.
- The organic sulphur compounds present in dates make it more significant in treating various seasonal allergies. A study conducted by Department of Nutrition, Central Michigan University, has revealed that this compound improved the symptoms of allergies.
- Packed with nutrients, dates are also consumed to improve the overall health of hair, skin, and to avoid premature ageing. Vitamin A, vitamin C, vitamin B1, vitamin B6, iron, magnesium, calcium, and phosphorus act as anti-ageing compounds.
- Dates also effectively increase the levels of iron in the body, thereby preventing or treating anaemia. They also improve the vigour and vitality of an individual.

Nutritive Highlights

Dates are high in calories, delivering around 310 calories in a 100 gm. They are an excellent source of antioxidants (like carotenoids and phenolics) and dietary fibres. They are rich in minerals like iron, selenium, potassium, copper, manganese, phosphorus, calcium, magnesium, and B-complex vitamins—thiamine, i.e. vitamin B1; riboflavin, i.e. vitamin B2; pantothenic acid, i.e. vitamin B5; niacin, i.e. vitamin B3; and folic acid, i.e. vitamin B9. They are extremely rich in carbohydrates as they consist of:

- 73 per cent sugar
- 5 per cent protein
- 9 per cent fat

Health Mantras

'It is health that is real wealth and not pieces of gold and silver.'
—Mahatma Gandhi

An individual can seek true sense of enjoyment from anything in life only if they are healthy. It is the healthy state of mind and body that defines the well-being of a person. The desired healthy state is pillared on four aspects—healthy diet, regular workout, disciplined lifestyle, and implementing few beneficial diet tips.

We are all now aware of the benefits of a balanced diet, regular exercise, and controlled lifestyle. But beneficial diet tips are either ignored or society is not much aware about them. So, what are these tips all about? The health tips mentioned below are nothing but few principles of doing certain things—associated with food—in an appropriate manner to gain all of the benefits for overall well-being.

The Elixir of Life—Water

One should start their day with drinking a glass of lukewarm water. It kick-starts the metabolic activities, cleanses the body, and improves the digestive system. It also helps in eliminating toxins more effectively. Drinking water that is stored in copper utensils in the morning has several benefits such as:

- Increases metabolic rate
- Helps in detoxification
- Raises haemoglobin levels
- Helps in weight maintenance
- Improves digestive power

One should make sure to drink water in sitting position. Drinking water while standing can disturb the fluid balance in the body, due to which the fluid can deposit in the joints, leading to arthritis after a certain age. Drinking water while sitting actually keeps arthritis and joint pains at bay.

Drinking water in while standing also allows water to fall into the stomach, creating problems not only for the stomach but the intestinal walls as well. It doesn't reach the organ it is supposed to and this leads to an accumulation of impurities in the liver and kidney. Also, make sure to drink water sip by sip, never in one go, to make maximum saliva dissolve in water and reach the stomach. It should never be gulped down without pausing. The human body is made largely of water—almost 70 per cent—so one should keep their body properly hydrated. It is essential for the cells to survive.

Moreover, water should never be consumed while having a meal or just after it. This is bad for the digestive fire, and people start encountering digestion problems, which usually leads to constipation. It is advised to drink water, at least, 45 minutes prior and 1 hour post a meal.

Lastly, drinking cold water, right out of the fridge, in any season is not good for health as it cools down the digestive fire, which, in turn, results in digestive issues. The body's energy is involved in bringing the cold water in the stomach to body's temperature, which would otherwise have been used to digest and breakdown the food that was consumed earlier. Drinking cold water also weakens the internal organs over a period of time.

Don't Forget about Milk

Undoubtedly, milk is a complete food, loaded with almost all nutrients. Actually, two schools of opinion exist in context to when milk should be consumed. Few are of the opinion that milk is heavy as it is loaded with protein and fat, and consuming it during the day makes the individual feel sluggish for the rest of the day. The other school of thought is that it should be drunk at night as it acts as a laxative.

Milk is also gifted with a sedative feature as it contains serotonin—hormones that reduce anxiety and depression—so it is best to have it during bedtime as it promotes sound sleep.

When milk is consumed while sitting, it passes half the body at a normal speed and then slows down and covers the rest of the body at a slower speed. In fact, it gathers in the lower section of the oesophagus due to the disruption. On the other hand, when milk is consumed while standing, it doesn't face any hurdles and easily moves down the body. The bloodstream picks it up immediately and carries it to all parts of the body instantly, which helps in obtaining all the nutrients that are present in milk.

Swallow Your Saliva

Our saliva is alkaline in nature and a boon to humankind. It has several medicinal properties and should be swallowed rather than spitting it out.

Morning saliva has the maximum benefits. Drinking lukewarm water helps swallowing the saliva thoroughly. It helps in fighting hyperacidity and acidosis. It improves and rejuvenates the digestive system as well. Produced in salivary glands, it consists of almost 98 per cent water along with other significant substances like amylase, antibacterial compounds, electrolytes like sodium, potassium, chloride, calcium, and phosphorus. It is associated with the task of moistening the food and swallowing it easily. Amylase breaks down the starch particles into simple sugar—maltose and dextrin—which facilitate smooth digestion.

Never Skip Your Breakfast

The digestive power is at its best in the morning—three hours after sunrise. So, whatever we eat during this period gets digested easily, prepares us for the rest of the day, and keeps us energetic. Due to these factors, breakfast should be the heaviest meal of the day and must not be skipped . . . ever. This is the time to consume the heaviest food as it can be digested easily, providing us with the nutrients required to perform our daily activities.

Add Slaked Lime (*Choona*) to Your Diet

Slaked lime is a great source of calcium. It needs to be consumed in a very small amount, i.e. just 2 gm per day. It can be consumed by sprinkling a little bit in a glass full of water and adding just a tablespoon of the mix to your dough for flatbread. After a certain age, the body's capability to digest calcium decreases, leading to calcium deficiency. Calcium helps in absorbing many micronutrients (minerals and vitamins) in our body. In the state of a calcium deficiency, micronutrients are not absorbed properly, which, in turn, leads to several issues.

Choosing Food According to Their Nature

Certain foods are warm in nature while few are cold. So, while selecting foods for consumption in winter, foods with warm nature must be selected like jaggery, dates, and ghee. Whereas, during summer, foods such as curd, buttermilk, cucumber, and bael should be preferred. In other words, foods that are seasonal should be preferred as they are fresh and most nutritive and favourable to body.

Cookware

Our health is not determined just by the quality of food we consume, but the cookware we use also plays a crucial role in defining our health. There are certain cookware that are responsible for stripping the nutritional value of food, and in some cases, making it toxic. If the cookware is reactive, it may lead to toxins in our food that are detrimental to our body, thereby leading to health issues in long run. Hence, safe and appropriate cooking utensils are vital in keeping one healthy. The selection of cookware should not be based on just durability and low price; in fact, it should be based on the benefits it provides to humankind.

Clay Cookware

In modern times, the use of pressure cooker has increased tremendously. But cooking anything in a pressure cooker destroys all the essential micronutrients. According to Ayurvedic Scholar Maharishi Vaghbhata, only 13 per cent micronutrients are left in dal cooked in a pressure cooker. As per the holistic guidelines, food that is cooked open has access to natural sunlight and air, which is highly beneficial. So, avoid using pressure cooker for cooking dal, red kidney beans, etc.

Cooking dal in clay pot yields 100 per cent micronutrients; even in brass and copper pots it is somewhat around 90 per cent. This decrease in nutritive value has been found in a lab research conducted by the CDRI (Central Drug Research Institute), Lucknow. As per Ayurvedic research, clay has 18 micronutrients that are transferred to the food that is being cooked in it. The food cooked in clay pots is enriched with minerals such as magnesium, calcium, iron, sulphur, and phosphorus. All these micronutrients are beneficial for our health. Clay has alkalinity that reduces the acidity of food, thereby resulting in neutral pH value and making food much healthier for us. Moreover, cooking in a clay pot requires less quantity of oil, making it more desirable.

But stay away from glazed clay pots that are readily available in the market as they have harmful substances like lead and mercury. Only unglazed and authentic clay pots are recommended for cooking.

Aluminium Cookware

Aluminium has the nature to be heated quite quickly, which reacts with food substances that are acidic in nature. Such chemical reaction affects the immune system and is not a desirable utensil to use for cooking.

Cooking in aluminium pots have been a cause of several diseases such as Alzheimer's, dementia, autism, and even cancer. Non-anodised aluminium cookware reacts with both acidic and alkaline foods and is considered to leach metal very slightly in food, making them dangerous for our health. Hence, acidic food such as tomato and alkaline food such as those containing baking soda should be avoided from cooking in aluminium cookware.

Stainless Steel Cookware

Stainless steel is basically an alloy made of chromium, nickel, silicon, manganese, etc. The best part is that food-grade stainless steel cookware is available in types 302 and 304. It is good for cooking food and doesn't harm us.

Cast Iron Cookware

Cooking in iron pots or *kadhai* is quite beneficial for our health. This practice adds iron in food, reducing the chances of anaemia.

Non-Stick Cookware

Non-stick cookware has been popular for a long time now and has become a household item. The non-stick character is due to the coating of polytetrafluoroethylene (PTFE). This material is also popularly known as Teflon and consists of carbon and fluorine particles.

Earlier, in place of Teflon, a harmful chemical called perfluorooctanoic acid (PFOA) was used. It was banned due to its potential threat to kidney and liver diseases. Teflon coating provides great comfort in preparing certain dishes that tend to stick on the surfaces of pots and pans with very little oil. But it has been proved that Teflon, when heated to around 300°C, exudes poisonous fumes. At this temperature, the Teflon coating breaks and releases toxic gases and smaller fragments of chemicals, which are dangerous as they are carcinogenic.

Teflon coating, once scratched with a sharp material, turns into a potential health hazard.

Trivia

- When an individual exercises, neurochemicals called endorphins are released in the brain that generate a sense of happiness and elation. It is said that exercise is equivalent to antidepressants.
- Exercise boosts sex life as well. In women, it leads to enhancement in arousal, whereas in men, it decreases the chances of erectile dysfunction.
- With age, the human head shrinks and degenerative diseases like Alzheimer's have a higher chance of occurring. Exercises carried out between the age 25 and 45 decreases the chances of the deterioration of hippocampus—a complex part related to the nervous system that is crucial for memory and learning.
- The human brain releases a neurochemical called dopamine as result of any kind of pleasure activity, for instance working out, having sex, or consuming drugs, alcohol, or food. Dopamine is a sort of addiction and makes people slaves of drugs, alcohol, or even sex. On the other hand, exercise helps in the recovery from addiction and distracts one from consuming drugs or alcohol.
- Antioxidants: Prune (dried plums) contains 7,291 antioxidants, whereas black plum contains 4,873 antioxidants.

- One cup of blueberries contains 13,427 total antioxidants, whereas farmed blueberries contain 9,019 antioxidants.
- In our body, water exists in various crucial forms such as plasma (colourless fluid of blood or lymph where fat globules are suspended), cytoplasm (material within the cell), serum (protein-rich liquid that separates when blood coagulates), saliva (watery liquid secreted into the mouth), nasal secretion, cerebrospinal fluid (fluid related to brain or spine), urine, and sweat.
- The lactose in milk is not digested by everyone easily. This is due to the deficiency of an enzyme called lactase in the body. The inability to digest lactose is called lactose intolerance. It leads to digestive problems like bloating, abdominal cramps, gas, and diarrhoea. Aspergillus is a fungus that has probiotic characteristics, and it helps in facilitating the breakdown of lactose. Aspergillus is available in liquid form and just a couple of drops can help ease discomfort.
- Orthorexia nervosa is an eating disorder that involves an unhealthy obsession with healthy eating. This condition is especially marked by the food quality rather than its quantity.
- A small quantity of freshly grated ginger with a dash of lime juice and salt activates the salivary glands, thereby producing essential digestive juices that facilitate digestion and proper absorption of food consumed. This easy-to-adopt mantra helps spark the digestive fire.

- Metabolism is a process that involves various chemical reactions to sustain life activity. It basically does three things—converts food consumed into energy to perform various cellular activities, transforms the food consumed into nutrients, and facilitates the elimination of waste. People either have high metabolism or low metabolism. In high metabolism, one burns more energy while performing activities and at rest, whereas one with low metabolism burns less energy. Hence, one with high metabolism may not easily gain weight even if she/he eats more than the one with low metabolism.

- The process of digestion, according to Ayurveda, has been categorised into three phases. First phase starts one hour after the meal is consumed. Here the kapha energy becomes prominent and makes the body feel full and heavy. The second phase starts 2–4 hours after eating a meal, and here, pitta energy takes charge. During this period, the digestive juices are released heavily, raising internal heat, and the meal is converted into nourishment. Last phase starts 4–5 hours after a meal wherein vata energy takes charge by giving lightness to the body and helping it regain the appetite.

  Any kind of hurdles in the digestive cycle leads to indigestion, and over a period of time, it results in the formation of ama in the body, inviting all kinds of disease and ailments.

- When anyone is dehydrated, their body is unable to eliminate impurities from the lymph system. Eventually, the blood flow and its production is badly affected as well, resulting in its inability to carry oxygen and nutrients desired for smooth functioning of the body.

- The belly button is, undoubtedly, a magical spot in our body that has been used as a source to treat many day-to-day issues. The navel is the first part that is created by the Supreme Almighty after the child is conceived. The navel (or umbilicus) connects the mother's placenta (navel cord) through the umbilical cord. Belly button is of importance as all the veins are connected to it. It would be a strange thing to believe that the part behind the navel is connected with more than 72,000 veins. Whenever oil is applied on the belly button, it is absorbed by the veins attached to it. Depending upon the nature and character of oil, it treats and cures certain ailments.

    - Neem oil helps in removing pimples and painful acne
    - Almond oil boosts radiance
    - Mustard oil relives dry and chapped lips
    - Olive oil or coconut oil improves fertility
    - Sesame oil strengthens the bones and reduces joint pains
    - Lemon oil helps in reducing face pigmentation
    - Mustard and ginger oil together improve digestive issues and treat bloating and nausea as well
    - Castor oil relieves knee pains
    - Pure ghee softens the skin
    - Warm ghee strengthens immunity and digestion along with improving blood flow to the nervous system. It also cures constipation

- Alcohol-dipped cotton ball cures cold, flu, and a runny nose
- Brandy dipped cotton ball eases menstrual cramps

➢ Nowadays, microwave is in every kitchen and is generally used to reheat food and hot beverages. Food in the microwave is heated with dielectric heating. While microwave is functional, the water molecules rotate with rapid frequency in both the food and the microwave, creating molecular friction and heating the food. This process changes the molecular structure of the food, decreasing its nutritive value.

➢ It has been researched that the one consuming milk and vegetables heated in the microwave experiences a decrease in the red blood cells and an increase in the white blood cells. It also changes cholesterol levels. Thus, it is apparent that microwave alters the constitution of one's blood. It has also been found to weaken the immune system due to its ionising radioactive waves.

➢ Mostly, plastic containers are used as bowls to heat food in the microwave. When plastic containers are heated, certain toxic chemicals—like benzene, toluene, and BPA (bisphenol A)—enter the food. These chemicals are carcinogens, exposing one to cancer.

➢ Allergen is any substance that causes an allergic reaction. This is due to a release of compounds called histamine in the body. Examples of allergens are pollen (a powdery substance discharged from the male part of a flower), small particles of dust, mould spores (a minute fungal filaments), latex (milky fluid that comes out from the cut of plant), wide variety of foods, insect bites, and several medicines. Allergen results in problems such as runny nose, itching, sneezing, watery and red eyes, skin rashes, asthma, shortness of breath, swelling in certain parts, etc. The problems may be subtle or harsh depending on the reason for the allergic reaction and on the immune system of the person exposed to it, too.

Some anti-allergic foods are:

- Apples: Quercetin, a flavonoid found in apples, is capable of stabilising cell membranes and prohibiting the release of excessive histamine in the body, thereby acting as anti-allergic food.
- Turmeric: Curcumin, an active ingredient, has the power of an effective antioxidant and is an anti-inflammatory as well, which helps in combating allergies.
- Green tea: Blessed with anti-inflammatory and anti-histamine properties, it has a compound called Epigallocatechin gallate (EGCG), which blocks the cell receptor that produces allergic responses.
- Lemon: It is an immune-boosting ingredient, which is loaded with vitamin C that helps in preventing allergies.
- Flaxseeds: The omega-3 fatty acids and selenium present in it works towards preventing allergic reactions.
- Sweet potatoes: It is a food ingredient that has a lot of antioxidants and can boost the immune

system along with halting histamine production. It is a great anti-allergic food.

- Ginger: It is an effective anti-allergic food that has anti-inflammatory qualities and works even better than some anti-histamine drugs.
- Garlic: It has been able to restrict the activity of inflammatory compounds, hence, preventing allergic reactions.

➢ Optimism is also a great diet! An individual with a high level of optimistic behaviour has better eating habits. This is easily visible from their lifestyle. Optimism rewards one with outstanding health and longevity.

Bibliography

1,2-vinyldithiin are organosulfur phytochemicals formed in the breakdown of allicin from crushed garlic.

Acetaldehyde is an organic chemical compound, which is found in foods like coffee and bread.

Alginate is a natural polymer found in brown seaweed.

Alkaloids are found primarily in plants and are a class of naturally occurring organic nitrogen-containing bases. Examples of alkaloids are morphine, quinine, and nicotine.

Anthocyanins are commonly found in flowers and fruits of several plants. Most of the red, purple, and blue flowers contain anthocyanins.

Arabinose is found in nature in the form of hemicelluloses and pectin. It is used to create cell culture in our stomach.

Beta-carotene is an organic, strongly coloured, red-orange pigment found in carrots and other plants.

Betaine is a modified amino acid found in wheat, shellfish, sugar beets, and spinach.

Betalains are water-soluble pigments found in beetroots.

Biotin is water-soluble vitamin H, which is found in foods like eggs, fish, meat, sweet potatoes, mushrooms, cauliflower, avocados, and nuts.

Carminative, also known as carminativum, is a herb or preparation intended to either prevent formation of gas in the gastrointestinal tract or facilitate the expulsion of said gas, thereby combatting *flatulence*.

Chlorogenic acid is a phytochemical found in coffee and coffee beans.

Coagulation is the transformation of proteins from a liquid state to a solid state on the application of heat. The protein coagulates in the range of 71°C to 85°C losing moisture, shrinking, and becoming firm and solid.

Cortisol is a steroid hormone regulating immune response and metabolism.

Curcumin is the bright yellow chemical found in turmeric and is a great health supplement.

Duodenum is the first part of the small intestine. It is located between the stomach and the middle part of the small intestine.

Ellagic acid is a natural phenol antioxidant found in foods like pomegranates, blackberries, strawberries, and walnuts.

Ellagitannins are a diverse type of tannins, a type of polyphenols.

Emblicanin A and B are a type of polyphenol found in Indian gooseberry (Amla).

Endothelium is a single layer that lines the inner surface of blood and lymphatic vessels.

Enzyme is a protein substance produced by a living organism that acts as a catalyst to bring about a specific biochemical reaction like digestion of food.

Epicatechin is a flavonoid that is found in fruits like apples, black berries, grapes, pears, raspberries, cocoa, and tea leaves.

Ergothioneine is an amino acid found in mushrooms, red beans, and black beans. It is used to treat joint pains, heart diseases, liver damage, and cataract.

Flavonoids are a type of substance found in some plants such as tomatoes that is thought to protect against some cancers and heart diseases.

Fructans are fructose polymer found in foods such as bread and pasta; onions and other shallots, cabbage, broccoli, barley, pistachio, artichoke, and asparagus.

Fructo-oligosaccharides are chains of plant sugars obtained from asparagus, artichokes, and soyabeans. They are used as low-calorie, alternative sweetener used for treating constipation.

Galacto-oligosaccharides are chains of plant sugars found in dairy products, beans, and root vegetables. They are used to treat stomach disorders, constipation, and allergies in infants.

Galactose is a carbohydrate that consists of two sugars from galactose and glucose. It is obtained from milk sugar (lactose). It helps in the brain development of children.

Gallic acid is an antioxidant found in foods like grapes, mango, strawberry, plums, walnut, tea, and wine.

Gelatine is a colourless, flavourless food ingredient, commonly derived from collagen obtained from animal parts.

Geraniin is a type of ellagitannin.

Glutathione is an antioxidant comprising three amino acids—glutamine, glycine, and cysteine. It is found in foods such as onion, garlic, avocados, watermelon, and asparagus.

Histidine is an amino acid. It is used to treat arthritis, allergic diseases, ulcers, and anaemia.

Homocysteine is an amino acid found commonly in our blood. It is obtained from meat flesh.

Inulin is a type of sugar, also called fructans. It helps in normalising the colon by being fermented by bacteria.

Isoleucine is an essential amino acid. It is found in foods like eggs, fish, poultry, meat, cheese, lentils, and nuts.

Isomalto-oligosaccharides is an artificial sweetener used in preparing bakery products.

Kaempferol is a type of flavonoid that is found in a wide variety of plants and plant-derived foods such as spinach, broccoli, beans, and tea.

Ketones are produced in the liver from fatty acids during the periods of fasting, restrictive carbohydrate diets, and starvation.

Lactosucrose is a polysaccharide and is used in the preparation of functional foods.

Lactulose is a synthetic sugar and is used to treat stomach disorders like constipation.

Leucine is an essential amino acid. It is found in dairy, soy beans, and legumes. It is the only amino acid that is associated with stimulating muscle growth and preventing muscle decline due to ageing.

Lutein is a vitamin that is soluble in fat and is found in foods like egg yolks, broccoli, spinach, corn, orange, kiwi fruit, grapes, and zucchini.

Lycopene is a plant nutrient that gives red and pink fruits their colour. It has been linked to various health benefits ranging from heart health to protection against sunburn and certain cancers.

Lysine is an amino acid obtained from food and is found in eggs, fish, meat, dairy products, and some plants like soy and legumes.

Mannan-oligosaccharides is a prebiotic made up of complex carbohydrates. It improves colon health.

Mannose is a type of simple sugar found in fruits like apples, oranges, and peaches; and vegetables like broccoli, cabbage, and beans. It helps in boosting metabolism.

Methionine is an amino acid that is found in fish, meat, and dairy products. It plays a key role in many cell functions.

Palatinose is obtained from beet sugar and is a low-calorie sweetener. It is used to avoid dental caries caused by sugar consumption.

Pectin is a unique, soluble fibre found in fruits and vegetables. It is a gelling agent.

Pepsin is the chief digestive enzyme in the stomach, which aids in breaking down proteins into polypeptides.

Phenylalanine is an essential amino acid. It is naturally found in the breast milk of mammals.

Ptyalin is a form of enzyme amylase found in the saliva of humans.

Punigluconin is a polyphenol compound and is found in the barks of pomegranate and amla.

Quercetin is a plant pigment found in foods like apples, red wine, onions, berries, honey, raspberries, citrus fruits, and green leafy vegetables.

Raffinose is a polysaccharide found in beans, cabbage, asparagus, broccoli, and whole grains. It acts as a dietary fibre.

Rennet is a complex set of enzymes produced in the stomachs of mammals and is used to curdle milk while making cheese.

Riboflavin is vitamin B2 and is found in eggs, green vegetables, milk,and other dairy products, mushrooms, almond, and meat. It helps in breaking down protein, carbohydrate, and fat to produce energy.

Rutin is a plant pigment found in certain fruits and vegetables. It is found in foods like asparagus, unpeeled apples, figs, black tea, and green tea.

Soybean-oligosaccharides are polysaccharides that are obtained from soybean. It helps in improving immunity of an individual.

Stachyose is a polysaccharide found in human milk and vegetables like green beans, soybeans, etc. It is used as a bulk sweetener.

Threonine is an amino acid found in foods like cottage cheese, fish, poultry, meat, lentils, and sesame seeds. It is used to treat nervous disorders.

Tryptophan is an essential amino acid found in foods like eggs, cheese, meat (especially turkey), wheat, rice, potatoes, and bananas.

Valine is an essential amino acid found in soy, cheese, peanut, mushroom, whole grains, and vegetables.

Xanthophylls are carotenoid pigments found in corn, pepper, egg yolk, meat of shrimp, lobster, and chicken.

Xylo-oligosaccharides are a type of sugar found in bamboo shoots, milk, honey, fruits, and vegetables. It is beneficial for the gut.

Zeaxanthin is a carotenoid found in foods like dark green vegetables, orange and yellow fruits, and egg yolk. It protects our eyes from the harmful effects of oxidation and light-induced damage.

Acknowledgements

Penning down a book is, undoubtedly, a gratifying and enriching experience. Many people have contributed a lot in accomplishing this task and I would like to pay gratitude to all of them from the bottom of my heart. In case, I missed someone's name, kindly pardon me.

I am deeply in debt to God, the Almighty, for giving me the strength and blessing to work on this project and providing me with the patience for the same. This book would not have been completed without the honest guidance of two mentors, Professor N. P. Singh and Mr Arun Kumar Singh.

My heartfelt thanks to Shailesh Singh, Seema, Inderjit Singh, Shailja, Mamta, Gaurav Amit, Shweta, Amit, and Rishi for their unending support and motivation. I would not have written this book without them.

Sonal, Sheetal, Kajal, Adityaveer, and Aaryaveer deserve a special thanks.

I also extend my thanks to Sonali Pawar, Vikas Mohan, Manu Vedant Saxena, and Dipti Patel for their support in making this book a reality.

I owe so much to my parents, my in-laws, and my wife, Sarita, for their unrelenting faith in me and this book.

I also owe a tremendous debt of gratitude to all those who have not been named here due to limitations but have, in one way or another, contributed in making this book a reality.